THE MULTI-HYPHEN LIFE

THE MULTI-HYPHEN LIFE

Work Less, Create More, and Design a Life That Works for You

EMMA GANNON

Andrews McMeel
PUBLISHING®

CONTENTS

INTRODUCTION

When it comes to your career, do you ever feel like you are on an endless journey to get somewhere and you never quite seem to arrive at the destination? This somewhere feels sort of like the sunny top of a mountain: You can't quite see it, but if you squint, you think you can see something blurry and special in the distance waiting for you. When you eventually get there—tired and exhausted—you assume everything will magically fall into place. You will eventually achieve career nirvana. It's what we've been promised. You were told somewhere along the way, maybe at school, that you'd reach this life goal in the end if you kept working hard, and it's the reason you toil away at work, nine-to-five (and then some), every day. We will get that reward, someday. When we get another promotion, another pay raise, another perk to post on Instagram, it will surely get us further toward this place of calm and satisfaction. "The dream." But what if such a place doesn't exist? What if, when you get there, there seems to be something missing?

On the way up and during those long hours at work, have you ever truly thought about what success really looks like to you? The daily small successes, the mundane stuff, the choices you make along the way? What if the success you were promised at the top of the mountain were to not feel or look how you expected? What if success has an entirely different meaning to each of us and we might be currently risking totally missing the point? What a scam that would be.

There are things we have to do, and unless you're extremely fortunate, work is one of them. But every single career guide I was given at school was outdated by the time I graduated. Even as recently as 2007, I was given the standard vet, teacher, lawyer multiple-choice brochure before I left university without any clue as to what was happening in the real world. In their defense, a realistic guide to an ever-changing modern working world can't possibly exist. For example, every single job I've had since graduating hadn't been invented when I was given those guides.

I also realize in hindsight that it wasn't only the act of picking a job that was frightening; it was the idea of picking one job for life. I was told and retold the myth that you can find your one dream path. I was encouraged to pick one subject to study, one subject to master. (Why do we have to "major" in something?) But successes in my career have come from having multiple projects, goals, and choices. You don't have to pick one job or be good at one thing. In fact, the positives and possibilities of living a multi-hyphenate lifestyle are endless, hence this book. Some of us—most of us—are not built to dedicate our lives to just one thing.

In Barry Schwartz's book *The Paradox of Choice*, he cites research that says having too many options can paralyze us into making no choices. But who says we have to choose? I wrote this book because I want us to break free from the stigma of being thought of as a "jack-of-all-trades, master of none" or the assumption that you cannot do many things well. It's possible to be good at many things! I've always been obsessed with multi-hyphenates: (Hanya Yanagihara, a bestselling novelist-fashion magazine editor; Naomi Alderman, a game designer-author-professor; Adam Kay, a scriptwriter-musician-writer; Nora Ephron, a director-columnist-scriptwriter). I love reading about people's "hyphens" and analyzing how they joined up together. It's led me to go on the hunt for real-life multi-hyphen stories. To me, a Multi-Hyphen Life looks and feels like a rich and exciting one.

My love and awareness of "hyphens" in my creative life have coincided with the rise in the gig economy, defined as "a labor market characterized by the prevalence of short-term contracts or freelance work as opposed to permanent jobs" by BBC news. It's predicted that by 2020 nearly half of all workers will earn some of their income from freelance projects. What's more, these freelance gigs are adding a huge amount of money to the US economy. As *Forbes*'s Brian Rashid says: "The old economy would lead you to believe that you should pick one job, work hard for the next 40 years at that company, and then retire. Not the new economy. The more diverse your skill set, the more opportunities come your way."[1] However, the freelance, or "gig," economy also has a bit of a bad rap: last-minute scheduling, insecure hours, zero-hour contracts. *The Multi-Hyphen Life* is not championing insecurity or project overwhelm, but it is taking into account that the gig economy trend on the whole is on the rise. Being a multi-hyphenate is about choosing and strategizing a plan of attack and having the freedom to take on multiple projects, not being backed into a corner. This is about choosing a lifestyle. This is about taking some power back into our own hands.

The multi-hyphenate lifestyle is about having a mishmash of projects going on with different income streams attached that make up a salary, instead of it coming from one source. Sure, it makes the "What do you do?" question harder to answer at dinner parties or friends' weddings, but your identity becomes less about what your singular job title is. It becomes more about who you are, what you are interested in, what pays the bills, and what your hobbies are. All these things make up your different "hyphens." You are a career chameleon, changing and molding yourself to different projects.

It's an important topic, work, as we spend so much our lifetime working, and even though it doesn't necessarily define who we are, it does make up a large proportion of what we do with our days. It would be irresponsible to pretend it doesn't matter. It matters because it's our lives.

So how do we thrive in a modern technology-obsessed work environment, cut through the noise, build longevity, and create our own definitions of success? How do we make ourselves happier and more fulfilled in a world that wants us to chase a never-ending finish line? How do we launch that side hustle that we keep talking about but feel like we don't know how to start? How do we stand out in a world where seven billion people are now joined in one interconnected online mass? How do we make money differently? How do we empower ourselves when we can feel so let down by an outdated system that doesn't work for so many? This book is my attempt to help you answer these questions.

The time frame needed for drastic change (in careers, lifestyle habits, technology) is shorter than ever before. We don't have as much time to sit back and figure out a new plan of attack. Even if we do, we feel the anxiety and strain of the future upon us. We are all thinking about our career 2.0. We cannot predict the jobs we will do in the future, but we can keep ourselves feeling secure in a new way. The impact of technology is not all positive, but it's allowed us to teach ourselves new skills, create new jobs, and build personal brands that over time attract consistent work.

The Multi-Hyphen Life is a practical look at how we can reinvent ourselves, the workplace, our environment, and our own definition of personal success, with a tool kit in chapter 7. It's about rethinking old habits and asking more questions. It's about designing our own schedules and not feeling limited to one thing or one box. In times of change, being really good at one thing isn't enough anymore.

THE MULTI-HYPHEN LIFE IS NOT:
  » a guide to being a blogger/model/DJ—sorry
  » a book just for Generation Z or millennials
  » celebrating the idea of insecure job-hopping
  » a guide on how to be a freelancer
  » a one-size-fits-all guidebook

THE MULTI-HYPHEN LIFE **IS:**
- » a look at how we future-proof ourselves in the new world of work
- » a reflection on the many ways we are being held back by workplace traditions of the past
- » a tool kit on how to be many different things all at once
- » a challenge to find new and personal definitions of success
- » a guide to use technology to empower us in our future careers
- » a new movement toward working less and creating more with your time

Technology has allowed us to rebel against what has been the norm for so many years. It has given us more freedom than we ever dreamed of. We can change our set parameters of the working day, use tools and machinery to tick off items on our work to-do list, and communicate with others around the world with a click of a button. The Internet has led to rises and falls too, for example: the fall of large-scale glossy magazines and the rise of our own curated magazines by real people on Instagram, the fall of traditional celebrity and the rise of Internet fame of the everyday person. We have the opportunity to start a business in our bedrooms without traditional funding, just with Wi-Fi, some online crowdfunding, and a good idea. Not everyone wants to be Mark Zuckerberg and conquer the world, but a lot of people want to give their idea a go, maybe even on the side of a day job. Because we can. It's about getting this balance right between learning how to use the Internet in the most efficient way and also realizing what we, as humans, can offer that machines can't.

And with new industries also come new gaps in the market. This also means embracing new job titles and realizing that your job could change at any moment. It's about learning how to pivot and adapt. Some job titles we roll our eyes at: happiness architect, culture guardian, emoji analyst, head of listening. But we just can't foresee what jobs will be popular in five, ten years, so the best option is to be continually open to change.

I often give talks and workshops, and I'm often inspired by people I talk to after, many of whom are launching their own side projects. I remember one workshop I did in 2016 that had such a huge variety of people in attendance, from an eighty-seven-year-old woman wanting to launch a website to sell her popular knitted items to a twelve-year-old girl who wanted to teach violin lessons over Skype to other twelve-year-olds in different countries. I believe deep down we are all entrepreneurial and capable of learning new skill sets all the time.

We've seen the demise of the job for life and the rise of the freelance economy. The gatekeepers are gone, and having so many more tools available online means we can create our own zigzag paths. We are finally asking ourselves, "Who made the rules?" when it comes to work. The average US office worker spends 28 percent of the working day on emails. Studies state that our portable inbox means the working day has increased from seven and a half hours to nine and a half. The Engagement Index study reveals that 42 percent of women believe it is increasingly difficult to disconnect from work while at home. Kristin Kelley, from well-known recruitment company Randstad, has noticed this: "On one hand, modern technology affords us to get more work done at a much faster pace as employees are able to connect to the workplace anytime, anywhere. On the other hand, the increased use of technology has led some employees to feel they are unable to disconnect from work, and that doesn't necessarily lead to greater productivity." Technology in many ways is making us work more.[2]

So our phones being in our pockets is not necessarily the answer to making work, work. None of this surprises me. Of course, there are upsides to working in an office: face-to-face meetings, bonding with colleagues, working as a team. But I also feel that I wasted time during the day in many different ways when I worked in an office: endless cups of tea, three different radio stations on at once, "Can I borrow you for a moment?" (when a moment turns into two hours), the aforementioned pointless meetings, unproductive delays, and commutes. All these things restricted me from getting things done. We work all day in an office and then work from our phones on the commute home too, meaning our working days are longer than they should be. So I asked myself: What could I achieve if I designed my working days from scratch?

I rebelled against the status quo of the traditional workplace because I felt disappointed by the inflexibility of many job roles that had no reason not to be flexible. Many companies seem so ingrained in having butts on seats and not taking into account our individual needs. Fast-forward to now: I have many different jobs. I am afraid I am unable to tell you what I do very easily. For a while, I felt like this was a negative thing—a lifestyle wrapped in stigma. A slashie (someone with multiple slashes in their job title) who couldn't commit to one thing. I would get tongue-tied whenever telling anyone what I did for a living. After years of mumbling instead of proudly proclaiming, I realized I wanted to write about it, and like most things that you think are your biggest flaws, they turn out to be your biggest sell. Once I embraced this way of working and gave it a name (the Multi-Hyphen Life, of course), my life changed, as did the quality of my health and relationships, my bank balance, and my idea of personal success.

The Multi-Hyphen Life has allowed me to have it all in a way I never thought possible. Sure, there are sacrifices, and there are important and complex questions to be asked about the future of work (see chapter 8), but I wanted to share my lessons and thoughts with you in this book. I wanted to write about how our home lives and work lives are merging now and how we can make that happen successfully and not burn out. Maybe you are feeling like you want a change, maybe you are braving the flexible working question, maybe you have a side hustle in you, maybe the job that once made you happy seems to irk you for some unexplained reason. Whatever your situation, I believe we are all multi-hyphenates deep down; we just need to be given the tools to make it physically work. We need a movement to join.

Perhaps your immediate thought is *Ugh, having multiple strands to my career sounds like more work.* But this book is not about having a to-do list as long as your arm and leg; it is about allowing technology to help us do less. Tech isn't going away, and we are still learning every day (which is a big theme of this book). Three decades ago, no one owned a computer in their home; now, according to research by Cisco, in 2008 there were already more "things" connected to the Internet than people. By 2020, the amount of Internet-connected things will reach fifty billion. And there's no sign of slowing down. Certain digital skills have the ability to lessen the workload and allow us to explore other skills that interest us. Having a side hustle is becoming a national pastime.

What if I told you that by adding many different hyphens to my career I actually work way, way fewer hours than my old nine-to-five job? Or that having multiple income streams can be a legitimate replacement for one sturdy salary? This book aims to break down the many stigmas of the modern-day workplace and explain why the hangovers of the past are ruining our chances to be fulfilled at work, keeping us feeling trapped, and stopping us from embracing our many sides. This book is about how everyone can have an entrepreneurial mind-set now and has the right to investigate it. Everyone. All we need are some tangible starting points to get our ideas off the ground, and we can create new jobs, not just for ourselves but for others. It's time to break off the shackles of the traditional restrictive workplace. Who made the rules that we had to live our lives so stringently and so straight? It's a new era, a new landscape, and a new time for new ways of working.

We also need to tackle the confidence crisis that comes with feeling like we are out there on our own battling through this era of change and forging new paths. The Internet has allowed us to hold down a job, work flexibly, create a new side job, and have a hobby if we want to, and with minimal travel requirements. But how do we make this a bigger conversation? Why are we still scared to ask for flexibility at work, and why is it still judged so harshly by many? After all, allowing ourselves to have multiple strands to our personality and careers allows us to mentally displace the weight and stresses of life onto different things instead. It's good for us. More on that later.

Recently, I've found myself having long conversations with part-time cab drivers who are in the middle of launching apps, while others are training to be pilots or writing books. I've met incredibly successful doctors: one who was training to be a videographer so he can be part filmmaker when up in the mountains saving lives, another who was doing heart surgery one day and blogging about food the next. This isn't about being forced into gigging by companies that don't care about us and won't invest in us; this is about choosing to have multiple sides to your work that you create and getting yourself into a place where you can take full advantage of all the opportunities that come with our new on-demand culture and economy. This is about having side projects that can be just for you. This is about empowering yourself at a time when we are becoming more and more fragile and disposable in the traditional workplace. It's about opening up these conversations and trying to make modern life work for us instead of driving us to the edge.

While being a multi-hyphenate is definitely not suited to just one generation, I couldn't help but be self-aware or at least self-analytical about where my point of view comes from as I wrote this book. I wonder whether being a millennial, fighting against the label of the "snowflake generation," and graduating during the recession of 2009—when job discovery and security were hard to come by—have become the driving force behind my work ethic. I felt like I needed a hustle on the side to make myself stand out because of the economic fear in the air and how competitive it was to secure a job. Because of serious issues like student debt and a housing crisis that has affected an entire generation, I didn't think of my career in a linear way because I knew I wouldn't have the same trajectory as my baby boomer parents. We are going to be working for a very long time, and the jobs that we do will continue to change and be continuously reinvented.

I also knew deep in my bones that technology was evolving at such a pace that humans weren't quite keeping up with it (or knowing yet the full capacity of what we could do with it). It felt like we were sort of running alongside it. I knew work and the workplace were going to look crazily different because of the rate of technology expanding and evolving in my lifetime and that I needed to invest in myself. If nothing was secure, then the only thing I could do was self-teach and invest in my own side skills. We should be taught the skills that will allow us to look at a landscape and see how it will change and grow and predict our own moves. We should be looking less inwardly when searching for a job or a career plan and instead look outward at our environment and our role within it. We should be less hung up on job titles and hierarchy and focus instead on what we can do and how much value it brings. A lot of things that used to be within a worker's control, such as steadily climbing up each rung of a career ladder, don't look the same anymore, so we can't control our next five years as much as we used to be able to. We should encourage ourselves not to be thinking of our careers in a linear way. We should be praised for asking "Why?" or "What if?" more often, instead of scorned.

Look, this idea of having multiple strands to your career isn't new. The portfolio career started to gain popularity in the 1980s, and then Charles Handy popularized the idea in his book *The Empty Raincoat* (1994). But it needs drastic updating and mainstreaming. The term "portfolio career" needs a modern twist that focuses more on tech, design, and the Internet, not just having a string of random jobs loosely held together. There wasn't a book for me when I started out, a book that combined growing a portfolio with enhancing your digital skills to carve out your own success and create a lifestyle that suits you.

We all have different names for it: interdisciplinary working, slashie career—my friend Freddie calls it multi-streaming—the art of having multiple income streams, pulling all the joint roles together like a puppeteer. Crucially, it's about making sure you do not become extinct in a workplace that is changing at lightning speed. It is diversifying yourself so that you are in the best possible position to have a long and fruitful career in a time where so much is out of our control.

I'm excited by all of this. The phone in our pocket has allowed us to daydream more than ever and connect with others effortlessly.

We see everyone else's pixelated magical life and business ideas and think to ourselves, *Could I do that?* On the Internet, we are constantly reminded of our own potential, and while it can be quite frightening (and sometimes overwhelming), it's also enlightening. The reason you get that fear-of-missing-out feeling when someone else starts their own business or project is because the playing field has been leveled by the Internet and you know that you could do it too. We are just as capable as Joe Bloggs. We all have similar opportunities for entry now and the same ability to spread our message. But talk of a digital strategy is missing, in a world that is becoming more competitive and noisy by the day. We need more conversations about resources and practical starting points. Not even that long ago, you would have to walk into an IRL bank and pitch your idea and ask for a loan. We don't need that kind of permission or investment up front anymore. We can experiment, take risks, and try something for almost nothing, and the world will not crumble if it doesn't work because we can try these things alongside our jobs. But the point remains that we are all free to give it a go.

The Multi-Hyphen Life at its heart is about being happier in walking our own paths. We've been told by society over and over again that it's totally normal to dislike our jobs. According to CBS News: "Of the country's approximately 100 million full-time employees, 51 percent aren't engaged at work—meaning they feel no real connection to their jobs, and thus they tend to do the bare minimum."[3] Bloomberg recently revealed that once you are over thirty-five, you're more likely to hate your job.[4] I met someone at a party recently, and when I told them I was writing this book, their response was, "But you're meant to hate your job. It's a job." I get it; no job is perfect all the time, but having multiple strings to your bow allows your life to be less weighted on one thing. Dispersing yourself and straddling multiple interests will make you better at each one because you are constantly improving and being challenged in multiple ways. You feel less trapped. You get to leapfrog over old barriers. It means you are giving yourself a break by embracing different parts of your life—personality and career.

I wanted to write a book that proves that anyone can leverage technology to bring in extra money or create personal value and how this can empower us. We just need to be given the tools to know where to start. We assume that if we are in a vibrant city, we are getting the most opportunities—and that is true of networking events—but you don't have to be a city-dwelling millennial to be an early adopter of new technology. You can create something interesting and engaging online no matter where you reside. This is its power. This is your potential for more freedom.

The Multi-Hyphen Life will offer you a different approach to your work life. It's the career guide I wish I'd had. This book is about making yourself more employable in an ever-changing and unpredictable world. It's about unpicking the stories we tell ourselves about who we are and our relationship with work. It's about overcoming any fears about it being dog-eat-dog online and offline. It's about playing to your strengths and defining your own success. It is going to bust the myth that there is only room for one job in our lives. It's about creating career longevity in a world and workplace that still have many hangovers from the past. It is about creating more stability for yourself, not less, so that you are employable not just over the next few years but the next few decades of unpredictability. It's about using one of the greatest gifts we've been given—the Internet—and working toward a flexible future.

Chapter 1

DICTIONARY DEFINITION OF SUCCESS VS. [INSERT YOUR OWN]

SUCCESS sək'sɛs/ noun
1. the accomplishment of an aim or purpose
2. the attainment of fame, wealth, or social status
3. a person or thing that achieves desired aims or attains fame, wealth, etc.[1]

In the dictionary, under the broad definition of "success," which is to "accomplish an aim or purpose" (makes sense, sure), there is also the more sinister definition that creeps into our culture: "a person or thing that achieves desired aims or attains fame, wealth, etc." It's this definition of success that we are fed in the media, on billboards, on TV, and in advertising, constantly. Internet memes and TV commercials still perpetuate the idea that we will be happier if we have more money, more things, more recognition, or more social-media followers. We will be a better version of ourselves if we get a bit famous! Or if we have loads of money, things, grand fireplaces, expensive rugs, gold, and jewels! I, like many people, I'm sure, fell into this trap at some point, thinking that all my problems would be fixed if I became "successful" in this way. This definition still lingers. Recognition and validation feel good. Initially.

But it's time to create a definition of success for ourselves. There are so many different ways to live your life, run your business, and earn your money. I am a multi-hyphenate, meaning that on paper I might not look as successful as someone who has a shiny desk in a tall, expensive building with a marble lobby. But having a multi-hyphenate career forces to create your own definition of success that can't be directly compared with others'. It's about carving your own path and staying in that lane. Your career mixture will look entirely different from someone else's, even if you have similar jobs. It's your bespoke package.

There are lots of things that are so ingrained in what we think success is that I have to force myself to inspect it and question it instead of just going along with it. *Is that my definition of success?* What do I actually want to do with my life? I can feel successful in the most mundane of moments, where I've made it through the day, not had any significant dramas, and then had a cup of tea on the sofa. I can also feel successful when I've been paid handsomely for my work. There are many different definitions of success that can apply to each of my individual career strands. It's up to us to start figuring it out, instead of chasing after the glamorized messages we absorb through media, be it social or traditional.

It's totally fine to have different definitions of success from your family, friends, peers, or strangers on the Internet. For example, I was recently pitched a guest for my podcast show (these sorts of pitches appear most days in my inbox, and I love hearing from and getting the chance to meet and interview new people whom I might never have come across before), and it had me scratching my head. The email read:

Dear Emma,
I have a suggestion for your podcast. We think you should interview X, an incredibly successful businessman who made so much money he retired at 26. Would you like to hear how he did it?

This jarred me, and I couldn't work out why at first. Was this the definition of success? Working and then retiring early? The thing is, it wasn't my definition. We are bought and sold success stories on a daily basis. We're constantly told that we should be successful and young. But no one is young forever. Success has no chance of surviving through your life if being young in your career is fetishized. Did I want to add to the gloss and romanticization of this idea of success? I am far more interested in discussing longevity—a life full of twists and turns and ups and downs and career changes. Balance. Fulfilment. Staying active. Enjoying life. Working a healthy amount. And, yes, of course, retiring (I hope) at some point! A corporate job and early retirement weren't my definition. To each their own. I knew I wanted to design a lifestyle that worked for me and not necessarily climb the traditional ladder, striving for promotion after promotion. I wanted to make sure I was having fun and fulfilling myself as I grew along the way. I wanted to enjoy my work, the challenges, the reinventions, the evolution, and the dance of a career and a life lived my way.

Kara Melchers, managing editor of BITE (a marketing trends agency), put it another way: "Our destination is not always reached by a ladder. In my head it's more like a climbing frame, one with tunnels and slides and ropes; as long as you're enjoying the journey, you're going in the right direction."[2]

Switching things up and trying new things are becoming more accepted, thankfully. I remember a boss at my old workplace telling me to stick each job out for two years; otherwise, you look unreliable to recruiters. Now I think that's less true. And even if you want to stay within a company, there are so many positives to taking on different roles within the building. A LinkedIn study by Guy Berger called "How to Become an Executive" analyzed the different ways LinkedIn members reached the top of their careers and achieved success in their roles. LinkedIn scanned data from 459,000 of their global members who worked at big consulting companies over a twenty-year period and were in senior positions. The study results showed that those who worked across multiple departments at one company were more likely to be in leadership roles than their colleagues who stayed in just one role or department. It showed that being adaptable and taking on different challenges can be a huge advantage in the workplace. It's important that we embrace this zigzag route as just as valid as the traditional career ladder.

In an interview in *Glamour* magazine, Adam Smiley Poswolsky, author of *The Quarter-Life Breakthrough: Invent Your Own Path, Find Meaningful Work, and Build a Life That Matters*, said:

> Changes in technology mean that people can't count on a position, or even a company, being around forever . . . Think of your career as a pond of lily pads spread out in all directions. This doesn't mean you should quit your job every six months for another lily pad, but it does mean that, to remain competitive, you have to become good at one thing, and then another thing, and figure out where those two skills intersect to add more value to your company.[3]

The Rise of Online "Success Porn"

If you've ever scrolled through social media and seen a trite motivational quote about "your grind" or a photo of an impossibly put-together office space with a marble desk and chic velvet chaise lounge posted on Instagram, you've seen "motivation porn" or "success porn." It's the way people try to get your attention by pornifying the idea of success, hyping you up, and making you want more—but with no real satisfaction at the end. There are over ten thousand uses of the hashtag #deskporn on Instagram, and it appears to be on the rise. One of my most disliked #workporn memes is the one that says "I'd rather hustle 24-7 than slave nine-to-five." It's shared on Pinterest a lot. The idea of hustling 24-7 is a really dangerous mentality to share, as working nonstop is not conducive to our happiness. We shouldn't be dividing our options into two extremes (i.e., nine-to-five = set hours vs. self-employment = working around the clock). There is a middle ground between working nine-to-five and working 24-7. We should work toward creating our own ratios that work for each of us.

If success porn in the fifties was a corner office, and in the nineties it was Steve Jobs quotes, then in 2019 it was the Instagram #GirlBoss running her empire from a beach in Bali. Although technology gives us the opportunity to carve out new career paths and side hustles, it can also bombard us with other people's "successes": someone else's successful kids, a successful real estate transaction, a successful job promotion, a successful relationship, a successful shopping trip. We are inundated with other people's lives. Or at least a very small part of people's public lives. Even though the Internet is responsible for a positive upheaval of our working lives, it is also the breeding ground for making us feel like everyone else is more successful than us. It takes a nanosecond to spiral into total compare-and-despair mode.

We can now access a new online world of endless pixelated lives and examples of success and make life choices based on what we see and think we want. We are influenced by so many more things now—there's a reason that social-media "influencers" exist. Tech has gone from being something we choose to use to something we cannot escape. To paint a picture of how quickly things have moved, in 2006 these things didn't exist:

» iPhone (and apps!)
» 4G
» Android
» WhatsApp
» Netflix
» Bitcoin
» Instagram
» Uber
» Snapchat
» Spotify
» Kickstarter

The list goes on. We are inundated with information. Slowing down and sitting back aren't just important for our mental and physical health; these crucial functions also allow us to see the forest for the trees. Are you really chasing your own "success" or someone else's?

Work Is Personal and Emotional

Work is an emotional subject for so many reasons. It can affect our mood, our perception of self-worth, and, in some cases, our health. Not everyone loves their job. In fact, if you do, you are the exception. According to global job finder Monster, 76 percent of workers get Sunday-night blues stressing out about the following day.[4] You're thought to be very lucky if you enjoy your job, but often the reality of finding yourself in a job you love is a result of many sacrifices along the way, often a low starting wage or working for free or "exposure" in order to stand out from the competition. In order to "do what you love," you might have to sacrifice job security, go without stability, and take a lot of risks. I was talking with friends of mine recently about just how controversial it can be at times to be the person who is happy at work. It can make things awkward in a friendship if you clearly love your job and your friends hate theirs. You may have uncomfortable conversations with friends who don't have the career they desire but might not want to take the leap or risk a difficult transition period either.

When I set out in the working world, I was slightly jealous of friends who were lawyers or in the finance industry, who enjoyed big salaries, luxurious holidays, and fancy restaurants right at the very beginning of their careers, whereas I was on the equivalent of $12K a year, living off tinned beans, trying to break into an industry I was passionate about but was known to pay pretty badly. Looking back, I don't know how I survived living in an expensive city like London, but I made it work on canned beans for lunch. But I soon learned it really is a waste of time comparing yourself with others when the decisions you made from the start were different. I had chosen to enter an industry that took longer to pay off. It didn't mean money didn't matter to me; it just meant I knew I wasn't going to get the same perks as my friends from day one.

It's more important than ever to have an understanding of the future of technology and the future of work so that obstacles can be examined more closely and we can overcome them no matter our background or starting point. The old-fashioned résumé, for example, used to be a way to manually filter who was and wasn't the right fit based on their educational and professional background. Now, the work can speak for itself, and instead of a résumé, your side hustle, special project, or website appearing on a certain Google search result could win you the job. According to a new CareerBuilder survey, 70 percent of employers use social media to snoop on potential candidates before hiring them. It's even got a name—social recruiting—and three in ten employers have someone solely dedicated to scrolling through the online profiles of prospective employees to find new, exciting hires based on their online credentials.

Educating ourselves, empowering ourselves with tech, and learning how to be more visible online or through new media (the growth of podcasts, for example, has meant a new voice or an idea can reach thousands if not millions of listeners without needing to go through the gatekeepers of radio stations) can lift up voices that used to not be listened to at all. We can all be more visible now. It's pretty great to have direct access to an audience.

SOME WAYS IN WHICH THE INTERNET HAS LEVELED THE PLAYING FIELD

- » We all have access to the tools to build the starting points of a business.
- » Anyone can build up an audience and communicate with them without relying on traditional media outlets.
- » Up-to-date tech and tools, on the whole, are accessible in most homes.

» In a time of change, companies and clients are willing to take risks on new, upcoming talent.

» Self-published audio has grown. For example, 51 percent of the US population has listened to a podcast.[5]

Being a Multi-Hyphenate Is About Building *Your* Own Definition of Success

"What I know now that I didn't know at 21 is that life is a series of dreams realized. There is no destination, but there will be breakthrough after breakthrough along the way. Our greatest obligation is to keep reaching, to continue growing, to push beyond what seems possible, to live outside the boxes created for us."

—ELAINE WELTEROTH, former editor of *Teen Vogue*[6]

A multi-hyphenate career means drawing on the things you find interesting and/or you are good at and creating your own career puzzle. It's like going into a career Build-A-Bear Workshop. This takes reflection and analysis of what you enjoy, where your strengths are, what you can build on, what you can enhance online, and, ultimately, what you can sell. The reason the multi-hyphenate lifestyle suits so many of us is because we don't want to fit into one box. We want to live lives that honor the different facets of ourselves—our complete selves.

Author Neville Hobson summed it up well on his website: "In a job-dissolving world, self-worth replaces identity."[7] We are losing our career identities because old status jobs are disappearing, so we have to find self-worth from other sources.

Status—and, therefore, "success"—used to be all about hours spent in the office, your expensive wardrobe, good hair, and how much money you earned. However, modern-day success can look very different. Minimalism—digital and real-world—has become more popular. The idea of material possessions being the definition of success is fading, with more people valuing experiences and memories (neither of which are created in meetings) over material goods. According to *Time*, millennials rank traveling and having experiences as a higher financial priority over the next five years than buying a car or home.[8] It suggests that there is an element of *we might as well spend money on enjoying ourselves if the economy is failing us.*

There is a tension between how the Internet can allow us to be individuals, explore our passions and interests, and tap into the tribes that share them with us while also being the largest breeding ground for buzzwords and trends, many of which are ephemeral or contradictory. On the Internet when something is "cool," it's easy to get sucked in. We start following and aspiring to a trend that we see others socially reward and validate. Trends like clean eating or extreme digital detoxing can take over the virtual space and can mean that we get easily confused about what it is that we actually want and what it is that actually makes us happy. Social media can be confusing— we aspire to lifestyles of "successful" people, but there's very little transparency around what those lifestyles demand or where they come from. We can see people posting about their global travels, but what is the day-to-day like? How is the travel funded? We don't see this sort of backstory on Instagram.

Our social and cultural idea of "success" over the years has been: Be good at something as a child, do well on your exams, go to a good university, get a stable job, get promoted, keep getting promoted, get a bit more money, get engaged, get married, have children, retire, die. (Fun.)

Or as David Brent (Ricky Gervais's character in UK edition of *The Office*) says: "You grow up, you work half a century, you get a golden handshake, you rest a couple of years, then you're dead."

Growing up, most of us are encouraged to be ambitious, but it's dangerous for success to be directly correlated to ambition.

And, of course, there are gender politics at play (when aren't there?). It's great that women are now seen as capable human beings in the workplace (wow, thanks!), but it's worth remembering that having the same opportunities doesn't always lead to equity. Despite widespread awareness of the issue, gender disparities in income continue:

> The gender gap in pay has narrowed since 1980, but it has remained relatively stable over the past 15 years or so. In 2017, women earned 82% of what men earned, according to a Pew Research Center analysis of median hourly earnings of both full- and part-time workers in the United States. Based on this estimate, it would take an extra 47 days of work for women to earn what men did in 2017.[9]

Personal fulfilment and feeling purposeful at work—which are emotional goals normally expected of women—can often be excuses for paying women less. It is assumed that women are more likely to be happy doing caring jobs over men, but many want (and deserve) straight-up cash too. According to OECD.org, around the globe women spend two to ten times more time on unpaid care work than men. It's no wonder that some women are opting out of traditional work when they get paid less for it and are still expected to carry additional care work for free.

And some women just don't want to be ambitious, just as some men don't. I have friends who admit (whispering like they are telling a dirty secret) that they have realized they just aren't that ambitious in the traditional sense, particularly when it comes to work. It shouldn't be seen as a bad thing to not be ambitious. I look at their lives, albeit different from mine (with babies, gardens, more free time), and I think to myself how much they have nailed their own versions of success. They are incredibly successful.

We all want different things, and that's OK. But we shouldn't be stereotyped into certain roles or have any decisions made based on gender. Success is personal.

Inward vs. Outward Success

"I was most taken by those who defined success as an action within their power instead of an achievement or desired state. Not perfection, but acceptance. Not self-love, but self-compassion. Not a win, but an effort."

—HALEY NAHMAN, Man Repeller[10]

In many ways we are incredibly lucky. If we were working in the nineteenth century, we might be forced into exploitive, unregulated industries, and our professional opportunities would often be circumscribed by our gender and background. Now we are able to forge new paths for ourselves, and technology and the Internet can help us be more productive with less labor.

One of the reasons I love being a multi-hyphenate is the variety of my days, from the variety of workspaces and travel I experience to the people I meet. Teamwork is important, but it has done wonders for my mental health to shake things up a bit. Anyone who works with the same people for decades might get bored or resentful or become complacent. Being a multi-hyphenate keeps me on my toes.

The idea of going into the same office every single day is quite old-fashioned, really. The traditional office space is a hangover from the Industrial Revolution too, when people had to be together for daylight hours to use machinery that wasn't portable. Even the apparently modern open-plan office isn't that modern. According to former millennial website The Debrief, the open-plan office is thought to have originated in Germany in the 1950s, from the idea of *Bürolandschaft* (office landscape). It was adopted by businesses all over the world and is now generally accepted as a utopian dream for businesses and their workers. However, after half a century of open-plan working, people are starting to question its benefits.[11]

The open-plan office gives the illusion of modern flexibility (with hot-desking purported to be a perk), but it is not nearly as flexible as it could be. For many, face-to-face contact with coworkers is still very important for relationship building, but in-person office work is not necessary for everyone. We don't all find the same spaces productive, but this is hardly ever taken into account. In one survey, 58 percent of high-performance employees said they need more quiet work spaces.[12] Another survey, conducted by Canada Life Group Insurance, found that people who work in open-plan offices took over 70 percent more sick days than those who worked at home.[13] With so many flexibility tools at our fingertips, why are set nine-to-five hours and a traditional office setup a requirement when we can do a lot of desk work from anywhere? When we can easily make up hours outside of the office from any location?

Another dysfunctional work habit that needs to die is workplace martyrdom. A workplace martyr is someone who is still at their desk at 10 p.m. not doing much, maybe watching a YouTube video, but complaining about how late it is and how long their to-do list is. But it's not impressive to be stuck in the office until 11 p.m. (I admit I definitely used to be that person!), and it's not an accurate measure of productivity or success. This is also referred to as presenteeism, which is described as "the practice of being present at one's place of work for more hours than is required" by theHRdirector.com. My opinion of what constitutes a successful working day has swung totally the other way: It is now getting good work done in the least amount of time.

It's interesting to look at the workplace martyr in different situations and different cultures. For example, in Japan, according to the labor ministry, few workers even come close to taking their full allotment of vacation time.[14] In South Korea it's encouraged to go for drinks and dinner with colleagues at least two nights a week. On average, because of this social requirement, South Koreans consume fourteen shots of hard liquor a week as part of workplace culture.[15] In the United Kingdom a lot of us are workaholics by nature and think that staying late can earn us brownie points from the boss. According to research by Fellowes, in the United Kingdom over half of employees go into work when sick, which is presenteeism at its worst. It's even more extreme in the United States. According to a US Travel Association survey, 41 percent of Americans don't take their paid time off, which is pretty alarming. By way of contrast, in the Netherlands it is frowned upon if you work late or don't take your vacation time. There, peers don't think, *Wow, you work really hard; you must have an amazing high-powered job.* They think, *What are you doing wrong?* Or, *You must not be very good at your job if you need to stay later than everyone else.*

These rigid definitions of success are way past their sell-by date. There is an alternative definition of success that isn't reliant on others' perceptions or old-fashioned ideas, and that is looking inward to find what living a balanced, enriched working life means to you. The Internet has created many different access points for us too. There's no right way to navigate toward your dream situation. We don't need to conform to old versions of success, however entrenched in our culture they might seem. We don't have to have one job for life. We don't have to choose one career path and stick to it. We can have any ratio or career mix. We can have multiple job streams; we can have side hustles; we can have many different definitions of who we are and how we want to live. We can step off the collective hamster wheel. It's OK if we can't sum up what we do easily; it's OK if we don't wow anyone at dinner parties with our job title; it's OK if what we do doesn't fit into the traditional parameters. If we are able to build a lifestyle that works for us, that's what's important.

What Success *Used* to Mean to Me

When I look back at what success meant to me as a young child, it was never about grades or gold stars. I think I was just lazy and was totally happy doing the bare minimum to scrape by. I almost thrived on the art of doing just enough. I never cared about praise from teachers or academic achievements. I hardly ever got any certificates or trophies for being number one, but on the upside, it also meant there was no anxiety or pressure to maintain any sort of special title. There is often a pressure once you are successful to then maintain that success. In my childhood eyes, it definitely made more sense to be mediocre at something, and then you don't get people's expectations set too high. If you did, you were sure to disappoint someone later down the line. Turned out that not being competitive is an easy way to get by and reduce anxiety. I actively avoided most classroom competition and instead chose to remain happily average. I was the same with board games. I would see someone getting dramatically competitive and richer than me over a game of Monopoly, and I'd just count my £1 notes. I just didn't care.

As I got older and into my teens, I started to develop a different definition of success, which for me was based on social popularity. It wasn't about being clever but having the most social attention. I would feel on a high and skip home if someone popular allowed me to sit next to them or gave me their last Rolo or picked me to be on their sports team. Social situations were always what made me feel successful. If I was invited to the cool party, I felt puffed up; if I was offered a cigarette by the older cool kids, I felt like a million dollars. In some (thank goodness healthier) ways, this is still my definition. I never feel more successful than when I'm surrounded by good, interesting people at work or friends I've kept close to me for decades.

When I moved to London at twenty-one, I expected to plod along. I was just happy that I was in London and managing to survive and stay alive in one of the world's most expensive cities. I wanted to be a writer, but that could wait. I just wanted to get any job, be OK at it, and go home on time. That was enough. But then that started to change.

My side hustles and my blog began taking off, I started to get invited to the "in" parties, and people began to tell me I was successful. The thing is that being seen as successful through other people's eyes (and not necessarily your own) can be addictive. You are rewarded if you become successful by society's (often shallow) standards. It's especially easy to get wrapped up in the online validation of likes and comments. We know that getting online attention can be as addictive as dopamine. Likes and comments feel just as good as sex, drugs, and a really good hug. I became obsessed with getting more and more positive feedback on my successful personal brand. It started to empower me, control me, and sort of take over. I wasn't in competition with others; I was in competition with myself. I was in competition with the last successful thing I'd done. You start to chase your own tail, and keeping up with the unrealistic goals you start setting for yourself can be exhausting.

Fast-forward to now. What does success mean to me?

Someone said that success to them was having enough flexibility that you can take yourself to a midweek matinee performance at the theater. Freedom is important to me. People want to feel free, even if it's as simple as being left to do menial tasks your own way. When FlexJobs surveyed 2,600 office employees in 2015, the majority said they actually prefer doing their most important tasks outside of the office.[16] It's quite simple, really. Humans like being trusted and feeling free.

When I look back through my experiences, I genuinely feel successful when I think of the network of people I have around me. I have friendships that have lasted decades. I feel successful in that I have time: time to work on my relationships like any other project, time to reflect, time to travel, time to take an afternoon off. And I have enough money to live.

The ability to have more flexible work, to work on my own side projects, to add different themes and strands to my work and personal identity, and to get to use those playful skills that were lost once I became an adult have all added to my personal definition of success. From the outside, success can look quite small, but the personal rewards can feel ginormous.

What Does Success Mean to You?

Success. A word wrapped up with so many different connotations, ideas, subconscious preconceptions. Does success actually still mean what we've been told it must mean? How do we take back control and pinpoint our own definition to keep for ourselves?

Before writing down your own definition, sometimes reading other people's thoughts can inspire you. Success to me is . . .

ANN FRIEDMAN, editor-writer-podcaster (Generation Catalano)

"To me, success is having the ability and fortitude to say no to things that don't align with my values or interests and still maintain a high quality of life. Success also means being able to weather big changes—be they in my profession or my personal life—and remain true to myself (my needs, desires, and values) and to my loved ones. (I'm technically the oldest millennial, born in 1982, but I identify more with Generation Catalano.)"

ANNE T. DONAHUE, comedian-author of *Nobody Cares* (millennial)

"Success to me means happiness. Which I know is a slippery slope because it's easy to conflate success with wealth or recognition or any other factor you're not in complete control of. But I think to be happy is to be successful. And I'm not even sure what happiness is or what it means, but I think chasing that is healthier than chasing anything else."

SARA, hospice counselor-supervisor-baker (baby boomer)

"Success to me is about doing paid work that has meaning and allows me autonomy to decide how I work. There's an element of public recognition and knowing I am respected especially by my professional peers. I want to be paid enough so that I'm not constantly worrying about money and there's enough for a few treats. I always want another level to achieve and more things to learn. Success for me is not a destination but a state of being that requires maintenance."

ALEX, catering company founder (Gen X)

"At the moment success means getting the right work-life balance, which enables me to manage my business with the energy and passion required. I also feel that success can be as simple as still being in business! Catering can be a tough old game, and as long as I am in business and managing to make some money, I suppose I am successful! (Blush!)"

JERICO MANDYBUR, author-founding editorial director of #Girlboss (millennial)

"My definition of success used to be quite unconscious—do something you're good at until you get to the highest point you can with it. But as I approached my early thirties, I went through the typical millennial burnout experience: exhausted and unfulfilled. Now I see success as more of a state of mind. Feeling satisfied with your contribution, whatever that looks like, and going to bed (8 hours a night!) without a feeling of dread."

GEORGIE HUMPHRIES, property manager (millennial)

"Success is pushing above and beyond the boundaries, not only personally but also what society considers to be a certain level of success for people my age/for women(!). Being promoted to a senior level in a quicker time frame than others, being younger than other managers/directors, being continually promoted within a fairly heavy male industry, financial security, personal happiness, pride in what you do, and respect from those around you."

LIZZIE PENNY, founder of agency the Hoxby Collective (Gen X)

"Loving what I do and being true to my work style—whatever it may be at that particular time. I'm a big believer that everyone should be deeply passionate about what they do and fulfilled in their lives, be that their work, families, or hobbies. I think people being fulfilled in their work specifically will make for a happier (and also more productive) society as a whole and that people should keep reflecting and questioning what they do and how they work until they truly feel happy with it—it's never too late for a change. Everyone should also be able to fit their work around their lives rather than the other way round."

RACHEL, founder of headhunting agency (Gen X)

"Having the time to actually reflect on what I've achieved—if I was just constantly working and never taking a step back, then I don't think success would ever be attainable. It can come in so many forms, but often I don't realize what I've achieved unless someone reminds me, which is totally daft. They're like, 'Hey, you've got your own business with employees, and it's super cool,' and I'm sitting there like, 'Oh yeah!' Success can be a total pain in the arse, though, as the likelihood is that if you're an entrepreneur, you suffer from impostor syndrome and probably won't be able to take in what you've done. It might be a couple of seconds where you're happy, but then you are on to the next thing . . ."

KATE LEAVER, author of *The Friendship Cure* (millennial)

"I've been thinking about this a lot lately—and finding myself caring significantly less about my definition of success from, say, a decade ago. I seem to have recalibrated my ambition, and where it used to be about the big, classic signs of success like a very obvious career on TV/radio, it's more personal now, like doing cool stuff that makes me feel inspired. It feels like a more sensible, less frenzied form of success that I'm after now—more closely aligned to happiness and creativity than the appearances of great things. So success to me now is being engaged with awesome people I respect, getting to do work I care about, and looking forward to a long, interesting career (rather than getting somewhere big fast fast fast). I'm actually starting to grasp that I will be working for decades to come, so success needn't come in a hurry—it's more to do with having great things to do for a long time."

GRACE CAMPBELL, documentary filmmaker-campaigner (Gen Z)

"It really depends on the mood I'm in and how secure I'm feeling in myself. Sometimes, when I'm feeling comfortable in my body, and in life, I judge success on how happy I am while I'm working with people I get on well with, which is most of the time. But then on other days, when I'm mentally low, fearing death, and comparing myself with other people around me, I feel like I need to get nominated for an Oscar and a BAFTA all at once to prove to myself that I'm talented."

LIV PURVIS, writer-blogger (Gen Z)

"Ultimately being happy and the feeling of contentment. Not feeling stressed by my career and being able to put food on the table without a burgeoning pressure. It's also meant to be able to create my own career and support myself in a creative industry. Once it was all about numbers and keeping up with the Joneses, but I think as I get older, it's been easier to appreciate what actually makes me feel successful, content, and fulfilled."

Practical Exercises

What are your definitions of success? Write down how your definition of success has changed from when you were a child, to a teen, to an adult. What needs to change or be tweaked? What has more or less weight now on your overall happiness and satisfaction? What definitions have you gotten rid of? Which parts of your life make you feel like you're the most fulfilled? What part of your life makes you feel the most successful, and why?

Another good exercise is to write down a list of things that maybe look good on paper but don't matter so much to you personally. Write the list and then physically draw a line through each one.

The benefits of figuring out your definition of success and writing it down enable you to feel secure in your own personal definition that won't necessarily match anyone else's. It means you have a version to keep to yourself, which you don't ever need to share if you don't want to. It means you are less likely to compare yourself with others, because they might be on track to meet their version, but your actions may look entirely different.

How to make your own pie chart: The idea is to keep a list over a few weeks, or months, of all the things that make you feel balanced.

On days where you go to bed thinking "That was a good day," write down the things you did. It might surprise you how small the action or output might be—like cooking a good meal, hitting a deadline, buying a thoughtful birthday present for someone, spending time on your hobby, or getting a pay raise. Whatever it is, write it down. The key is to write down the things that genuinely make you feel good, not just what you think will look good on paper. Then, take all these, group them into categories (i.e., if you have lots of references to time away from your desk, perhaps this can become "travel"), and assign them a percentage of how important they are to you.

Keep this pie chart above your desk, stuck to your laptop, or in a notebook you use often so you are reminded of it. I reevaluate mine once a year. It gives enough perspective on what you have achieved and the ways in which you might have changed.

Here's mine (which is ever-changing, and that's OK too!):

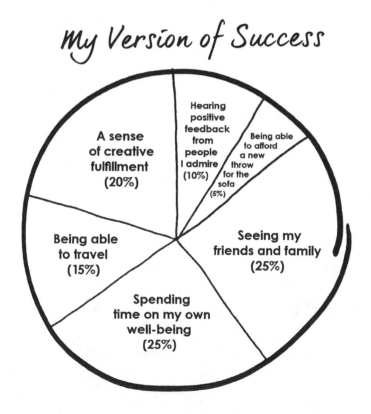

My Version of Success

- A sense of creative fulfillment (20%)
- Hearing positive feedback from people I admire (10%)
- Being able to afford a new throw for the sofa (5%)
- Being able to travel (15%)
- Seeing my friends and family (25%)
- Spending time on my own well-being (25%)

Chapter 2

GENERATIONS AND MOTIVATIONS

"It is one of the great ironies of life that each generation believes its experiences are unique."

—JOHN MAULDIN, financial expert and
New York Times bestselling author[1]

Different generations have always felt distanced from each other. The challenge is not to stereotype. But it's hard. Immediate stereotypes spring to mind as I type this. I can't help it: Younger generations appear threatening to me; older generations can seem wise but also intensely judgmental at times. But it doesn't make sense to be labeled and put into boxes simply based on the year we were born.

Those within the same generation each grow up with a slightly different set of circumstances but will always have some similarities with the people who were born around the same time. After all, we are all products of our environment and the economy we grow up in. But what are the generational differences? This chapter takes a quick and dirty look at the different generations currently in the workforce and how and when they came of age, which may inform some of their motivations and career choices and also how they define success.

Generational Overview[2]

BABY BOOMERS (1940s to mid-1960s)

Baby boomers—the result of the "boom" of new babies after World War II—are the first modern generation to, on the whole, do better financially than their parents. According to TheBalance.com: "in the early years of the boom, schools were overcrowded, colleges didn't have enough seats, and the competition for starting jobs was intense. As a result, the young Baby Boomers learned to compete for resources and success." They are also more open-minded and less obedient than their predecessors. "They are more optimistic and open to change than the prior generation, but they are also responsible for the 'Me Generation,' with its pursuit of personal gratification," according to training company Amanet.

GEN X (mid-1960s to early 1980s)

The label for this generation became popular alongside Douglas Coupland's book *Generation X—Tales for an Accelerated Culture*. Millennials grew up on the Internet; Generation X created it. According to a piece by David Barnett in the *Independent*: Gen Xers "transformed the Eighties and we owned the Nineties . . . had alcopops and ecstasy and we were fearless and stupid and happy, but we still got up for work on Monday morning, no matter how bad we felt."

MILLENNIALS (1980s to mid-1990s)

Millennials, or Gen Y, grew up with the Internet and were introduced to evolving technologies, from dial-up to smartphones. According to LinkedIn: "Millennials aren't as willing as former generations to sacrifice their personal life in order to advance their careers. They also expect a more flexible work environment than previous generations and want to work for a company that supports various causes."

GEN Z (mid-1990s to late 2000s)[3]

Gen Z is pretty new to the workforce, but its members have had all sorts of Internet hobbies for years, as they've pretty much always been online. They will most likely go into jobs that aren't yet invented and care about having a purpose and participating in social activism. According to entrepreneur.com, "they have also grown up in a much more accepting and respectful environment compared to those generations that came before."

A Few Obvious Generational Differences

Are the generations all that different? Baby boomers are now the fastest-growing group of social-media adopters, but my job didn't exist when my parents had jobs, so I can't ask for career advice because the job market changes so quickly, and they are, in fact, now retired. We differ in our relationship to university (my tuition—probably cheap by US standards—was expensive; my dad went for free), and the housing markets we experienced were different too. But our gap is much narrower in some ways than my dad's and my grandad's generational divide. I can talk to my dad about most things: He is tech-savvy (and can ask Alexa to play music from his Sonos speakers), he understands the struggles of my generation when it comes to the smaller details, and we have a lot of things in common. My dad's dad, however, of the Silent Generation (or "the Greatest Generation," which refers to the generation that fought in WWII), had no real education, left school at fourteen to work in a butcher's shop, then fought in the war and never, ever had a computer or a mobile phone. There are so many things he did that I will never be able to relate to.

So you could argue that the gaps between generations are becoming smaller. Are we more bonded because of the similar tech we use? Will the first digital-native generation (aka millennials) be closer to their digital-native children? It will be the first time a 100 percent digital native will give birth to another digital native, after all. We are moving in the same worlds, but there will still be divides because of how fast technology moves on.

Arguably, our working structures have remained pretty much the same for decades and decades, since before World War II. But when you think of just how much has changed between then and now, it's crazy that work hasn't changed in leaps and bounds to reflect that. The nine-to-five and butts-in-seats mentality still rewards loyalty over and above productivity. We still put face-to-face contact high on the priority list, even though we're technologically capable of connecting with one another from just about anywhere in the world. We are a million miles away from what the world used to look like, so how do we change up the face of work, especially for new generations?

Why Do We Keep Pitting Generations Against Each Other?

When any system has been in place for a long time, there are hangovers (and not the alcoholic kind) that we have to deal with. The residue of any old system still lingers even if it seems like big changes have been made over time. It can be messy and uncomfortable. The millennial generation and younger don't think too positively of the old rules of the workplace. Millennials experimented with and were early adopters of new tech for years before getting into the workforce, so perhaps we find it jarring when we can't put our niche digital knowledge to really good use and instead have to adhere to systems, hierarchies, and old structures. Millennials don't necessarily remember the good old days, as they graduated around the time of the recession and so weren't yet a solid part of the working world when print media was booming, or when the music industry was still thriving selling hard copies, or when we shopped only in brick-and-mortar stores. Perhaps this is why we are more adaptable and are happy to get on with things in new ways or start our own ventures from scratch. There's a lack of nostalgia for a more traditionally stable time we never knew, so we don't feel like there's much to lose. But it's not just millennials who want to change up the workplace or work in a multi-hyphenate way.

It's crazy to think we have at least four different generations at work right now, spanning from age seventeen to seventy. Of course, this will mean similarities and differences in work opinion, career history, and values. But cooperation in the workforce is all about appreciating each other's strengths and being open to new ideas and ways of doing things.

Many companies I worked at were brimming with new roles in digital departments, and at one point I found myself managing a team who were all five to ten years older than me, which I found challenging. I've also had bosses who are a lot older than me, and their insecurities shocked me. These situations made me see that no one felt totally secure in their roles, and I began to understand why there was tension. I found working in teams that were chosen for me could often be quite challenging. Other elements of my multi-hyphen lifestyle are that I get to pick my own bespoke team, I get to work with a wider range of individuals from different companies and with different areas of expertise, I get to work with people in other countries, and I get to cross-pollinate and brew ideas with people in coworking spaces.

Big-scale change is slow, and the workplace is just one example of that. Changes need to be made in the working world on a micro level, and this requires a big change in our overall mind-set too. Asking for big or small changes to your role or working setup is often still met with a raised eyebrow, with flexibility still thought of as a massive perk rather than something that makes economic sense for many businesses. Tech entrepreneur and Amicable app cofounder Pip Wilson agrees: "I believe the opportunities for flexible—and effective—working that now exist for everyone are greater than they have ever been. But a societal mind-set change is imperative."[4] If the number of new start-ups and multi-hyphenates keeps growing and the consistent rise in the gig economy continues, then it's increasingly important that this new flexibility is matched with protection and workplace benefits. It's a bigger conversation. It's a new system and structure that are needed, not just a quick tweak to the existing one.

Generational Myths

As George Orwell wrote: "Each generation imagines itself to be more intelligent than the one that went before it, and wiser than the one that comes after it."[5] We all think we are doing the right thing, but we have slightly different perspectives.

My grandfather owned a driving school, and just as he retired, people had started getting computers at work. He just missed the boat on the digital workplace. (And thank goodness! How BORING that would have been to painstakingly digitize decades of handwritten files when he was just a few years from retirement.) The practicalities and efficiencies of digital work are something we take for granted now. The idea of not having the Internet at work feels totally alien to us, but it's a relatively recent development, and even the most technologically literate of us are all still in learning mode and always will be as tech continues to evolve. Multigenerational offices can be interesting to navigate when older workers can feel overwhelmed by new tech and younger generations may struggle with workplace hierarchies or ways of doing business that feel outdated. The old system used to work. But a lot has changed in a very short space of time, and while many organizations pretend they are keeping up, they aren't.

It's time to bust some old myths.

"Our culture is currently obsessed with generational labels and the stereotypes that go with them," says Jessica Kriegel, author of *Unfairly Labeled*. "There's about 80 million Millennials right now and some of those Millennials are CEOs in Silicon Valley, and some of them are illegal immigrants in the Midwest who are waitressing somewhere," Kriegel said. "You really can't put them all in a box. And what we do is, we put them all in a box, and that box is really based on a middle-income, white, American person and then we just say that's the only kind of Millennial that exists right now.[6]

"What really determines whether someone is frugal or if they want to save the world has to do with, did your parents feed you? Did you have an aunt that spoiled you? Did you have books in your home? Did you go to a good school? . . . There are a million factors that go into determining the kind of person you are when you grow up, and this arbitrary 20-year-long age bracket that is widely accepted is not one of them."[7]

Of course, there are bigger factors at play than just the year you were born. According to the Recruitment and Employment Confederation (REC), we are going to see big changes as "Baby Boomers decline as a percentage of the workforce offset by the growing influence of younger generations who place a higher value on flexibility, work-life balance, and personal development."[8] If these values really do matter to the younger generation, which study after study says they do, then we can expect the workplace to change quite quickly over the next decade.

Dismissive stereotypes of different generations aren't productive. Millennials aren't "lazy" or "entitled," for example. Really, the gap in understanding is caused by a breakdown in communication about changing wants, needs, and values in the workplace. Millennials and Gen Z may just want to live their lives differently—preferring flexibility when that's possible. The question should be: How do we cater to an increasingly flexible workforce across ALL industries? We have the chance to recalibrate what a working day looks like in industries across the world and how technology and automation can contribute in a positive way.

It is also a myth that boomers aren't good with technology, just as much as it is a myth that all Gen Z are vacuous and totally obsessed with taking selfies. Baby boomers are often thought of as not being digitally savvy, but that's of course not always the case. According to a report by Google, baby boomers spend more time online than they do watching TV! They are more likely to share something on Facebook than younger generations. They've even been dubbed "silver surfers." Boomers also have the most disposable income and most of the property ownership, so this is a generation that can afford to upgrade their homes with the latest gadgets. When it comes to leading a multi-hyphenate working lifestyle, it is definitely not solely for one generation. Everyone benefits from flexibility, freedom, and finding new skills.

In studies as early as 2010, Nielsen released reports showing that boomers spend the most money on tech: "It's actually a myth that baby boomers aren't into technology. They represent 25% of the population, but they consume 40% [in total dollars spent] of it."[9] They also spend way more on online shopping than other generations on average, according to Forrester Research's annual benchmark tech study. The future of work affects all generations, and all generations are able to reap the rewards of how the Internet can offer flexibility and new job roles or side hustles.

Social-media use in the older generations is on the rise too. According to the Office for National Statistics, one in four over-sixty-fives are now using social-networking sites such as Facebook and Twitter. Dubbed the "Instagrans," the proportion of over-sixty-fives who say they are active on social sites grew by more than 50 percent last year.[10]

The number of over-seventy-fives using social media has nearly doubled in the past year, Ofcom has found, with over 41 percent of over-seventy-fives using it, up from 19 percent the previous year.[11] Boomers enjoy growing their social-media followers and upgrading their tech as much as Gen Z.

Tim Kellett, director at Paydata (a management consultancy), says all employees with diverse skills should be seen as an asset to their employer. "Employees are taking control of where and how they want to work, therefore employers need to be adaptable in order to retain such talent."[12] Instead of just pushing millennials and Gen Z aside as being entitled, it might just mean that employers need to adjust the workplace in order to keep their talent within the organization. Otherwise, employees will leave, maybe to start their own project or company, because they can.

In her piece for the *Atlantic*, "Have Smartphones Destroyed a Generation?" Jean M. Twenge wrote: "The aim of generational study, however, is not to succumb to nostalgia for the way things used to be; it's to understand how they are now."[13] This is the main thing: We shouldn't just ignore the past; we should try to understand our differences while also realizing our many similarities. We must move forward and accept the reality of now, instead of arguing about how things might have been better back in the day. We can't go back.

Where Are We Now?

When it comes to any sort of change, it's hard to have perspective on it when we're still in the thick of it. But it does feel like the past decade or so has dramatically shifted how we get information and how we express ourselves. The Internet has changed what we see. It's hard to tell whether we know too much, with everything at our fingertips, or whether we know nothing at all. As we've become more entrenched in our online worlds, we're experiencing massive shifts in trust, skills, connection, and culture.

THERE'S BEEN A CHANGE IN TRUST

We have trust issues. Trust in leaders and people in political power is fragile and weak. The Internet is full of information we think twice about retweeting because we question whether it's true. The Edelman Trust Barometer, a survey of over thirty-three thousand respondents across twenty-eight markets, is really interesting. It gives an indication on who trusts whom each year when it comes to the media, government, politics, etc. I remember when the trust back in the earlier noughties had shifted from "trusting the media" to "trusting people like yourself" and people started finding blog recommendations more trustworthy than TV commercials. Since then, trust in various institutions and figures has continued to decline. The 2017 Edelman Barometer revealed the largest ever drop in trust across government, business, media, and NGOs. Trust in media is at all-time lows in seventeen countries, while trust levels in government dropped in fourteen markets. The credibility of leaders is also in dire straits. CEO credibility dropped twelve points globally to an all-time low, plummeting in every country studied. Trust in authority is vanishing and is being replaced by trust in those most like us. The UK population trusts their family and friends over four times more than political parties and leaders.[14] I don't think it's a coincidence that there's a lack of trust in public figures. Lies are often exposed online, more information is available to the public to research and make sense of, and in the United States 88 percent of millennials "sometimes" or "never" trust the press. I think this has a lot to do with the rise of anxiety. The less we trust our external sources, the more we worry. If we don't trust the grown-ups anymore to sort things out, we take on that stress and anxiety in other areas of our lives. Without trust, everything can feel more up in the air and like it could collapse around us at any minute. Rebuilding trust, right now, is a matter of urgency.

THERE'S BEEN A CHANGE IN DESIRABLE SKILLS

I think a lot of crossed wires in the workplace are rooted in misunderstanding and fear of obsolescence, and that fear is understandable. In a recent piece for the *Guardian* in 2017, Yuval Noah Harari said that "by 2050 a new class of people might emerge—the useless class. People who are not just unemployed, but unemployable."[15] A lot of people will be pushed out of jobs because of automation and technological advancements in the workplace, like the use of robots and AI. He further posits that "no one knows what to study at college, because no one knows what skills learned at 20 will be relevant at 40." That is not a fun thing to read, but it feels very true. The challenge is to embrace these fears, create better working relationships, and be open to learning new skills throughout your working life. During a talk at the MacDowell Chairman's Evening while speaking about his mentor David Carr, writer Ta-Nehisi Coates said, "He had this wonderful ability to not be afraid of young people. He would completely and totally invest in young people." It reminded me of how many of my own bosses didn't necessarily try to lift their younger employees up or use their new skills to their companies' advantage, instead often trying to push them aside out of fear.

Younger workers often have an edge when it comes to new-to-the workplace skills, like leveraging new technology. I grew up believing that if the Internet was going to be such a massive part of my life, I had to also believe that it could help make my life slightly easier. The Internet has allowed me to shortcut my career. I have been able to give myself a platform in order to get more opportunities from many different corners. I've used Twitter to connect with employers, a blog to get more work, and the Internet to leapfrog my way into a hard-to-get-into industry. My full-time job in a corporate marketing environment wasn't moving fast enough for me because the company was too big to invest in my individual career goals, so I experimented with new tools on the side. If your job doesn't offer you interesting, exciting ways to up your game or try things out, you can still do it in your spare time. I read up on things, curated Twitter lists, signed up for RSS feeds, launched websites, tested my Photoshop skills with free trials, and realized that I didn't need to wait for some big company to train me—and even if they did, it would be months or years too late. I had to train myself. And the best part was I could do it in thirty-minute chunks in the evenings or on Sunday mornings over a cup of coffee. I started to enjoy teaching myself new things, regularly, calmly, and in my own time because it was never going to be wasted. The key is to stay curious and do it in manageable pieces of stolen time here and there.

THERE'S BEEN A CHANGE IN HOW WE CAN WORK

Not all jobs allow flexibility. But the nine-to-five genuinely baffled me, as someone who grew up learning basic coding skills, who knows how to schedule content to post online while I'm sleeping, and who has been able to multitask on my phone since age twelve. The notion of the nine-to-five working day was established in the Victorian era when no one really cared about the worker, so it's no surprise that it bewilders the modern generation. This is a generation that earns money from their bedrooms—because they want to (maybe) but also because they have to. It's confusing to have work emails on our phones 24-7 while we're simultaneously told to work a rigid nine-to-five. I was expected to answer my emails on the train into work, but if I was five minutes late, I would get death stares from all corners of the office.

In the 2001 book *The Body Clock Guide to Better Health* by Michael Smolensky and Lynne Lamberg, the lark and owl theory (something I've always believed in) is explored. "One in ten of us is an up-at-dawn, raring-to-go early bird, or lark. About two in ten are owls, who enjoy staying up long past midnight. The rest of us, those in the middle, whom we call hummingbirds, may be ready for action both early and late."[16] It's easy to understand why the nine-to-five originated—factory and office workers needed light, shelter, and face-to-face contact—and the majority of people are hummingbirds. But what about the larks and the owls? These differing body-clock types show that we don't all just fit neatly into one box or all work our best in the same way. Work flexibility should be more widespread; an hour moved here or there could have a massive positive change for some employees. We are so easily accessible now (perhaps too much so), so why not embrace it? I'm definitely an owl. The book says, "Owls often skip breakfast, and they're always rushing to get to work in the morning." Whereas give me a bit more time in the morning to get moving and I am an absolute winner at getting stuff done later in the day. We should be encouraged to figure these things out about ourselves early on at school (that and learning what taxes are), because your dream job could be dependent on your body clock: "If you're a lark, you probably wouldn't enjoy a job as a nighttime bartender. If you're an owl, you'd have a struggle to report the morning news."

In an article for *Fast Company*, entitled "How to Design Your Ideal Workday Based on Your Sleep Habits," sleep expert Michael Breus said you could be a bear (average sleep pattern, 50 to 55 percent of the population, with a morning routine of 7 to 11 a.m.); a lion (wake up without alarm, around 15 percent of the population, with a morning routine of 5:30 to 10 a.m.); or a wolf (hate mornings, represent 15 to 20 percent of the population, with a morning routine of 7.30 a.m. to 12 p.m.). With all this research into sleep patterns and productivity, why are we not embracing it more and using it to understand ourselves better and inform our workplace routine?

Flexibility is not just about digital millennial nomads with stickers on their MacBook Pros. We're talking single parents, people living with chronic pain, elderly workers, and the list goes on. We could all benefit from having some more flex in our lives and not feeling guilty about it either. Flexibility is also about productivity, because when someone is at the center of their own schedule, they can get more done. As Charles Kenny wrote in a piece for *Foreign Policy*, "The bottom line is that productivity—driven by technology and well-functioning markets—drives wealth far more than hours worked."

THERE'S BEEN A CHANGE IN WORK CULTURE

Workplace culture is hard to pin down, isn't it? I've been told in many job interviews that my résumé looks fine but what they really want to know is whether I fit in with the culture of the office. What is workplace culture exactly? Essentially, is it the character and personality of the organization. It is the people, the community, the vibe, and how you feel when you're there. The thing is I've worked at companies where the culture was incredibly fun and motivating (Friday-afternoon group presentations! Free ski trips!), but I was miserable. I felt ungrateful. I felt privileged. But I also felt like the perks weren't making me happy at work; they were actually making me feel more attached to my day job, more indebted to the office, more guilty if I wanted any sort of flexibility outside of it. Successful workplace culture can't be just based on perks. Culture isn't just about free beers on a Friday. It's not even free doughnuts. It's about how a place and people you work with make you feel.

I was interested in Twitter's new Culture 2.0 manifesto as an example of a company making positive change. In their New Work

Manifesto there were many statements that resonated with me including "40 hours is enough," "reclaim your lunch," and "digital sabbath," inspiring employees to "escape digital enslavement." It is a sign that even digital-first companies are encouraging more offline time to bond with colleagues and be happier and more fulfilled. Work-life balance has never been so important, and not just for millennials.

A study in 2016 by *Fortune* found that, on average, millennials would be willing to give up $7,600 in salary every year to work at a job that provided a better work culture and environment for them[17]—a sign that when it comes to working, our comfort and happiness in our surroundings matter and may affect our decisions more than money. Our working environment is important: office culture, colleagues, flexibility, comfortable workspaces, up-to-date technology, and feeling connected to a company's mission and invested in its success.

THERE'S BEEN A CHANGE IN WORKPLACE HIERARCHY

A global Deloitte study surveying more than seven thousand companies found that 92 percent of those surveyed cited organizational redesign as "the top priority." Josh Bersin, who worked on the study, suggested that people have less defined jobs and move laterally from project to project.[18] In most modern-day jobs (although not all), hierarchy has had to take a back seat or at least be restructured or reconsidered. Of course, there are many jobs where experience is the key factor (a surgeon, for example), but in the kinds of new roles that have only just been created, a younger generation of workers have self-taught, learned in-demand niche skills, and don't necessarily fit into a traditional hierarchy. Climbing the ladder is not so simple anymore.

Hierarchies don't work as well as they used to because the way we acquire expertise has changed. An expert doesn't necessarily look like a long-standing CEO, especially if they are removed from their company's day-to-day microdecisions. New industries and new ways of working are more likely to have niche experts who don't need decades of experience on their side to prove their knowledge. Expertise can have little to do with age or number of years spent in the field. You can be an expert on the very thing you are creating, designing new jobs that haven't existed before. It's a great time to have a niche and to own it. Broaden your horizons, add different hyphens to your bio, and capitalize on a time of huge change when a small idea can turn into something very big indeed. It is a time to not be intimidated by others and work toward creating your own expertise.

A myth that comes with the multi-hyphenate tag is that having a diverse career must mean you cannot be an expert because you are a jack-of-all-trades. But gone are the days where you must dedicate your entire life to one thing. So many jobs are still evolving that there is a whole wealth of brand-new industries, sectors, and niches that don't yet have any experts (could you become one?), and there are future jobs that don't yet exist (could you invent one?). Tech has opened up so many avenues to become an expert, by simply doing, experimenting, and teaching yourself. Now is the time to make your own expertise in a new area of your career. The democratization of online education and tools means that anyone can advance their skills and knowledge in a new area of tech without traditional training. By simply doing things enough times, you can pick up new skills. This is not about people being marginally good at a variety of things; it's about picking multiple skills to hone that complement one another. Adding that variety of knowledge, picking up new hyphens as you go, can be more fulfilling than the vertical ascent of a shiny corporate ladder.

It's important that companies learn to move more quickly and become more nimble. In a piece by Aaron Dignan, investor and founder of the Ready (a company that helps organizations redesign their structure), he said: "Even in a self-organized, decentralized, collaborative, and high-trust future (in fact, especially in that future), people will need to navigate their organization. Data will need to flow transparently and fluidly across the network. Roles and projects will need to be created, filled, and disbanded with increasing frequency."[19] This means that job titles potentially won't last as long. A company may be updating itself so often that we won't have the choice to feel married to our job title or job identity. We will move with the changes or get left behind.

That may be the case for the agile company of the future, but right now too many workplaces are bureaucratic and slow to adapt. It is another reason why a lot of people go it alone, start a side hustle, or invest in a project alongside their job, because they can do it more quickly without the layers of approval that exist in some companies. They can learn, grow, take risks, and experiment without needing sign-off from ten people every time. In some cases small projects built from scratch outperform established organizations; for example, a former start-up company like Airbnb now books more rooms than the world's largest hotel chains.[20] Having a creative hyphen outside of your day job can allow you to add to and experiment with the fast-changing skills that will be needed in a bigger company. Those skills can add to your job in many beneficial ways, or your side project could take on legs of its own. It's a win-win situation.

Be Inspired by the "Yes, and . . ." Generation

When we think about teenagers now, in many ways they grow up more quickly—embracing technology, learning about things online, having Google at their fingertips for any questions they might have. This comes with its downsides, of course, but I believe the Internet can be largely educational. In an interview with *Coveteur*, Phillip Picardi, chief content officer at *Teen Vogue*, said, "Teens are very much the 'Yes, And . . .' generation. They're always on top of new things before you are and you always have to keep that in mind."[21] Of the ways young people connect online, Scott Hess (a seeming multi-hyphenate himself, on LinkedIn he lists his job title at media agency Spark as "Executive Vice President (Corporate Marketing, Generational Intelligence) also: poet") said: "These guys are actually together by voice on gaming networks, and visually on Skype or Google Chat as they do their homework together. It's still virtual interaction, but it's full sight, sound and motion rather than just texts."[22] This constant connection leads to creative idea generation, information sharing, community building.

Gen Z know they are worth more in the marketplace, so they expect more flexibility and bigger paychecks. Millennials were slightly different, beginning to carve out change, but mostly still followed in the old steps of the baby boomers: Get a good education at school, earn a degree, chase a corporate job, and get on a ladder. Tech and social media hadn't become as ubiquitous as the basis for viable careers yet—millennials didn't quite know what they could do with them or the extent of them. For example, hugely successful YouTubers such as Zoe Sugg aka Zoella and Louise Pentland have both stated they felt vulnerable leaving their full-time jobs to pursue "influencer" careers, a concept that was brand-new at the time. Zoella famously says her dad told her to get a "real job" when she was just starting out. It hadn't been done before. The path the baby boomers took hasn't worked in the same way for younger generations, and jobs and skills are evolving so quickly, and perhaps this is why they have embraced the Multi-Hyphen Life.

A lot of Gen Z creatives aren't even entertaining the corporate handshake; they're multi hyphenates from the get-go. In fact, according to Daria Taylor, cofounder of Talented Heads, a digital-marketing agency, "We'll see more of this generation not going to university because of the high cost, but going straight into the workplace—and maybe doing some online studies." It appears that Gen Z are going to go straight into the thick of it. University curriculum could be out-of-date by the time they graduate, and with the accessibility of independent learning and the opportunity to build an online platform, a traditional educational and career trajectory may be less productive. This means that a lot of Gen Z have to take their own risks, find their own paths.

It's very easy to just brush young people aside as being narcissistic, but it's unfair. The reality is that in our crowded, increasingly connected world, if you don't foghorn your achievements, you can't expect to have them recognized. And younger generations are putting their digital know-how to good use. As Phillip Picardi says: "This is not just the selfie generation or selfish millennials, this is an audience who is uniquely engaged in changing the world by being involved in social justice."

It feels like, on the whole, most of us do want to have some sort of positive impact. Publishing, activism, and building our own entrepreneurial empires online often come from a place of caring about the future. Because the gatekeepers have changed, and in some cases crumbled, we don't need to have a traditional platform to have our voices heard. What is the price we pay for this opportunity, though? On management guru Tim Ferriss's popular podcast, tech executive Seth Godin said something that spoke to me:

"Social media wasn't invented to make you better. It was invented to make the companies money. And you are an employee of the company, and you are the product that they sell. And they have put you in a little hamster wheel, and they throw little treats in now and then. But you gotta decide: What's the impact you're trying to make?"

If social media is just a hamster wheel and we are making Internet companies money by using it, then it makes sense to try to get something out of it, to have some impact along the way: impact on our own lives, impact on our friends' lives, and impact on the world around us. Finding out who we are matters. Having a strong sense of self matters. Having a purpose matters. Don't be afraid to have multiple careers and interests.

What Actually Motivates Us?

So, reflecting on this change in culture, skills, and trust over the years, what actually motivates us? It's interesting that a big part of our lives now does not feature on Abraham Maslow's hierarchy of needs pyramid. Maslow's seminal 1943 paper, "A Theory of Human Motivation," posits that humans have physiological needs (air, food, shelter, sex, sleep), safety needs (security, law, order), love needs (friendship, family, trust, love), esteem needs (dignity, independence, respect from others), and, finally, self-actualization needs (seeking personal potential and growth). We in the Western world live in a privileged society where most of us don't have to spend as much time on basic primitive survival, so we can spend more time on our self-growth. Maslow's pyramid was created in a time when 80 percent of workers still worked in a factory.[23] It seems as though Wi-Fi and social media would definitely be added to this pyramid if it was reimagined nowadays.

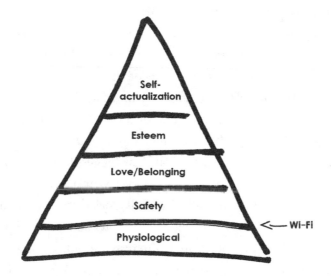

One of the stereotypes about younger workers is that we're good with the Internet but really bad at holding down a job. But there are deeper reasons behind why many of us don't commit to one job, and they have nothing to do with the fear of hard work. The world is currently changing at breakneck speed, and millennials and Gen Z are adapting and taking advantage of their niche set of skills. And maybe the confidence to take risks results from having less to lose. For example, millennials have taken on at least 300 percent more student debt than their parents,[24] so they are already on the back foot financially. They are also less likely to own property and more likely to have kids later, so why not take a chance on a side hustle that you enjoy and that might even bring in some extra cash?

The kinds of roles available to workers have drastically changed over the past few years. My job as social-media editor did not properly exist even five years ago. I was told off for going on to Myspace (one of the earliest social networks, now defunct) at school when, just like many others my age, I was teaching myself how to code for the first time. Since 2010, social-media positions are up 1,357 percent on LinkedIn.[25] Studies from the BBC World Service say that "65% of jobs haven't been invented yet."[26] (It might not come as a shock that nearly 70 percent of parents admit they don't have a clear understanding of their children's jobs).[27] In 2008, there were zero big-data architects (people trained to describe the structure and behavior of big data) on LinkedIn.

And what do the newest members of the workforce, Gen Z, expect from their jobs? According to data by Randstad, Gen Z are 5 percent more likely than millennials to work for themselves (37 percent to millennials' 32 percent).[28] Money may also have a different meaning to Gen Z, 46 percent of whom say that their biggest financial concern is student debt, which has increased year over year in the United Kingdom and the United States especially. Not only does Gen Z want employers to allow them to use social media and other tech in the workplace but also many of them are increasingly interested in integrating emerging technologies, such as wearables, virtual reality, and robotics. It is also interesting that 45 percent of digital-native workers want to have a career in technology, a number that continues to grow.

But, for many people, especially the younger gens getting started, it's difficult to target a single profession you want to go into. According to Jean-Philippe Michel, an Ottawa-based career coach, workers "need to shift from thinking about jobs and careers to think about challenges and problems."[29] He believes, like me, that we need to "prepare the next generation for a career in the future, which for many will be made up of numerous micro-jobs aimed at well-paid skilled workers, and not a single boss and company." New generations of service providers have sprung up to connect niche workers and companies who need them. The Hoxby Collective, a consultant group, handpicks "a team of specialists from around the world specifically for your brief; bringing together only the finest talent, only when you need it." YunoJuno is a company that connects experts and multi-hyphenates to the job or microjob remotely. The Dots, a United Kingdom–based company founded by Pip Jamieson, which TechCrunch called "the LinkedIn for creatives," is a network that connects freelancers in fashion, the arts, and technology to new clients and recently raised £4 million in funding. These sorts of companies and services will continue to rise, helping flexible workers get the job done productively, with the business on the other side getting the benefit of the best, most talented experts for the job.

Today, driven by tremendous volatility in the job market, we change jobs often. And it's across all generations now. The average baby boomer will change jobs 11.7 times in his or her career, according to a Bureau of Labor Statistics study, and millennials change jobs every two years or less.[30] So how can companies make themselves attractive to a more mobile workforce? According to a study by HSBC, 89 percent of people surveyed by the bank (of all ages) said the thing that would motivate them to be most productive at work is flexibility. This was then followed by remote working and then (lower on the list) things like a bonus scheme, training opportunities, extra sick days, and health insurance.

We are all evolving and adapting faster than we are given credit for. Whether baby boomer or Gen Z (and all of us in between), we all have unique strengths and the ability to design careers that may not have existed a decade ago. It's important to make sure generational barriers don't get in the way of working together, especially when it comes to building the future of work. We all love a sensational headline, but we are much more similar than we think.

Practical Exercises

What about you? What motivates you? What makes you excited to wake up? What is it that drives your hunger and ambition? Only when you know and understand your key motivations can you work backward in order to create your own definition of success.

Some days go by in a whirlwind, and I don't get the chance to understand why on that day I felt motivated. But what I try to do is make a list of the smaller moments when I'm feeling motivated and then try to unpick them by asking questions such as:

1. Was my personal life affecting anything?
2. Do I respond better to certain physical environments?
3. What sort of people motivate me?
4. What sort of people drain me?
5. Are there days I enjoy more than others?
6. Do some days feel easier than others? Why?
7. What days excite me the most?

Try this exercise yourself.

With the responses to these questions, what answers are you left with? Visualize all of your answers by drawing your own spider diagram, like mine below.

Chapter 3

THE RISE OF THE
MULTI-HYPHENATE

"You are not only one person! But dozens, hundreds of personalities! But boy you might never meet all of them! We try so hard to fit into boxes, that we end up suppressing some of what we are and end up living the wrong lives."

—FREDDIE HARREL, global fashion entrepreneur[1]

The Multi-Hyphen Life is about being a happier and more fulfilled person at work and otherwise. It's about breaking out of a predetermined definition of success that may no longer be viable. But it also doesn't necessarily involve leaving your day job. This isn't a "quit your job"-type book. It's also not about labeling yourself a "freelancer" and telling you to go it completely alone. The Multi-Hyphen Life for you could mean nurturing an outside-of-work hobby—or hyphen— that complements your interests and adds to your skills. A side project doesn't have to mean world domination or a global business plan.

The Multi-Hyphen Life is the straight-up refusal to be pigeonholed or afraid to add another strand to your career bio. It is rebelling against being (a) defined by what generation you fall into and (b) mindlessly following someone else's path. You are not your job title and instead should feel confident enough to move between different jobs if necessary, relying on your strategic personal branding to funnel, organize, monetize, and schedule your work yourself. This is not about having fifteen jobs, juggling to make ends meet, tearing your hair out at night. It is an active choice to have more than one job, a career with multiple strands that suits you.

We shouldn't assume that freelance flexibility and multiple career strands mean exploitative "gigging." *Flexibility* is far more preferable—the happy medium between a single full-time nine-to-five and unsupported gigging. There is a vast and varied spectrum of options in between these two extremes. According to the Office for National Statistics in the United Kingdom, at the beginning of 2016 the self-employed accounted for 15 percent of their population. That's 4.6 million people who could do with more advice, tools, resources, direction, and opportunities for work. With institutions notoriously slow to evolve, we have to take charge of our own career paths. The Multi-Hyphen Life is about taking that control: harnessing multiple skills and housing them under one career roof.

THE MULTI-HYPHENATE LIFESTYLE IS ABOUT . . .

» allowing yourself space to breathe
» allowing yourself to not be defined by a box that having one job—with a title chosen by someone else—can put you in
» having the courage and tools to make big moves on the side, without risking financial stability
» giving yourself the confidence to not be defined by one thing
» letting go of thinking your job is your life, your identity, and your worth
» letting yourself add other names and titles to your bio as you go
» letting your hobbies and outside interests make you better at your job
» having two simultaneous careers or more—whatever ratio works for you
» allowing technology to help you live a happier, more creative lifestyle
» getting rid of obsolete traditions of the past

Your hyphens don't even have to be work related to make a difference. Your hyphen could be "parent" or "caregiver" or "poker champion" or "chief knitter" or "flash mobber." Your hyphen doesn't have to make you money. It can be an enjoyable bonus and outlet alongside your job. Of course, additional income is amazing and can be a welcome by-product of having multiple projects, but it all starts with incentive, intention, enjoyment, and curiosity. This is a new age of employment. You manage your own training, create and maintain your job security, and build your own online ecosystem. You are running your own business—the business of you—with a mixture of skills to offer.

YOU CAN BE A MULTI-HYPHENATE *AND* . . .

» have totally different interdisciplinary careers. They can look dissimilar on the surface but complement each other in interesting ways.

» still be an expert in one or more areas even if you have multiple interests or hyphens to your job title

» not be overly ambitious! Having a multi-hyphenate career isn't always about being the best or being the hardest hustler. It is about having a cocktail of projects and work that makes you feel satisfied and driven.

» still maintain a successful day job or part-time job, with career strands added on the side. The beauty of this lifestyle is you don't have to pick just one way of working.

It's Time to Be Unapologetic

I used to apologize for everything. I would just be sorry all the time. I would apologize if someone spilled their coffee on me. I would apologize for taking up any space, breathing air. And I always felt the need to apologize for my lifestyle and career choices. For years I have apologized for how I work and when I work. I used to run my side projects from home in the evenings and was met with judgment from colleagues and acquaintances (perhaps because I looked like I was a crazy person, trying to build a moonlight side business on no sleep). I asked my employer whether I could have Wednesday afternoons off so that I could finish writing my first book. It felt like a momentous ask, because it wasn't really the norm. I'd leave the office on Wednesdays at 1 p.m. and write from when I got home at 2 p.m. until 6 p.m. Four solid hours of side hustle time. But before leaving the office every week I would apologize guiltily, make an awkward joke, and sneak out while everyone else was tapping away. The thing is I'd asked for and been given the flexibility I wanted. So why did it feel like I was committing a weird crime? Why did I feel like some of my other colleagues were side-eyeing me? Why did I feel guilty that I wasn't using this flexibility for a more "acceptable" reason, for example, for childcare? Whatever my guilt surrounding my decision, those four hours a week dedicated to my side project ended up sparking my career trajectory and added nicely to my finances.

Sometimes we have to take risks and be unapologetic for the things we want. It can feel awkward at the time, but later you'll be glad you pushed through. Do you have something you wish you had more time to do? Even the smallest amount of time to see whether it's feasible? Do you think it's time to ask your employer for the flexibility to try it out?

In June 2016, I was selected to act in a national TV commercial for Microsoft. It played in theaters and in the breaks of shows like *Britain's Got Talent*. In the thirty-second clip, I say: "Millennials will have more than five jobs in their lifetime, and I think it's very exciting." This sentence was born out of the Chase Jarvis quote: "If our parents had one job, we'll have five, and the next generation will have five at the same time."[2] Many viewers perhaps didn't fully get it. How can you get a complicated premise about the future of work across in just thirty seconds? I love the commercial and the conversations it sparked, but I knew I wanted to discuss this in more detail.

I was selected to be in this commercial because I am a technology-obsessed and self-defined multi-hyphenate in the workplace. I have always been someone who could never put herself in a box, and for years this made me feel insecure. But when a huge technology brand wanted to showcase my career story on a national platform (TV, theaters, all over the Internet), perhaps it was the validation I needed to realize that this way of working is something to be taken seriously.

This idea of what is now safe is interesting to me in this changing world of work. Can any job really be that safe these days? The job-for-life scenario with a great deal of career and retirement security that many of our parents and grandparents had no longer exists for us. But we all want and deserve to feel secure in our jobs. People ask me these questions a lot: Don't you feel unstable? Don't you miss your monthly salary? My answers: One, I felt more unstable working for a company that I didn't believe could keep up with the technology revolution (I thought some of my old workplaces were likely to fold, and some eventually did). And, two, I do make a salary, just in a different sort of way. I feel much more secure and confident knowing that by having multiple skills, I have a diverse digital résumé, and I'm more employable. The future looks unpredictable, so how can we pretend that sitting at a nine-to-five desk is stable or secure?

We are all entrepreneurs now. The very meaning and idea of what an entrepreneur is have changed (it's not just start-up founders in Silicon Valley; it's you, it's me, it's anyone sitting at their kitchen table with an idea), and the playing field has been leveled. In my head the idea of an entrepreneur was always someone in a suit, pitching in a board meeting. Rid yourself of the idea of what you think an entrepreneur looks or sounds like. Those old ideas are fading fast. If you have a smartphone or a laptop and an idea, you can be entrepreneurial. You can start an online marketplace, launch an Instagram page, sell tickets, make a podcast, or grow an attractive online portfolio. As Muhammad Yunus, the Nobel Peace Prize–winning microfinance pioneer, pointed out: "All human beings are entrepreneurs. When we were in the caves, we were all self-employed . . . finding our food, feeding ourselves. That's where human history began. As civilization came, we suppressed it. We became 'labor' because they stamped us, 'You are labor.' We forgot that we are entrepreneurs."[3]

We are told that some of us have an entrepreneurial mind-set and some of us don't, but I don't believe that's true, just as I don't believe that only some of us are creative. We are all creative. We are all entrepreneurial. You just have to decide whether to put it into practice or not.

It's OK to have different things going on. The common denominator is you. You are the person who stitches it all together. Juggle, grow, explore, and then whatever happens to our working world or whatever technology is next invented or whatever the new trends are, you will have everything you need to adapt and pivot. This is about giving yourself the permission to have more control of your choices and future.

It's Time to Start a Side Hustle—for Your Bank Account or Just for Yourself

A side hustle has been defined as "a low-risk project, meaning it shouldn't take a lot of start-up capital."[4] Essentially, it's something that encourages you to learn new skills or enjoy a passion project that doesn't take a lot of up-front investment in time or money. It isn't strictly work or play but something in between. Technology has broken down the traditional barriers to creating a viable side hustle— giving more people access to tools and resources than ever before. It's important to stay curious about the future of tech and keep our technical knowledge as up-to-date as we can so that we don't end up with a huge imbalance of skills. Feminist author Caitlin Moran has discussed the gender imbalance that already exists: "If you look at the stats on coding, it's still crackers isn't it? [The latest research says 92 percent of software engineers are men.][5] . . . That's like if the global language was going to be Chinese, and women weren't learning Chinese. The future is tech, the future is coding, this is how we build the world, this is how we understand ourselves."[6]

Side hustling is not just a trendy turn of phrase; it is a genuine add-on to many workers' lifestyles. According to research by GoDaddy,

48 percent of Britons who start up a side business do so to make money from a passion or a hobby, with some entrepreneurs reportedly earning between £500 and £5,000 on top of the salary from their day job.[7] In the United States, according to Bankrate, one in four millennials have a side hustle, with 61 percent of millennials working a side hustle once a week or more, 96 percent at least once a month, and 25 percent earning $500 a month or more from their side hustles.[8]

It's clear we want to shake things up a bit. In the United States, as many as 81 percent of traditional workers surveyed said they would "be willing to do additional work outside of [their] primary job if it was available and enabled [them] to make more money."[9] That's a huge number of people who would be willing to have multiple jobs.

There are reasons to start small with your side hustle—you can gauge interest, assess whether it might be worth growing, and avoid burnout. Starting with a small amount of your time (like one hour a week) is a low-risk way you can put your creative energy into something outside of your day job and experiment with ways you might monetize your idea. Using your time wisely means you can grow things on the side without risking your primary employment.

My first side hustle came about because I hated my job. I was miserable. The work culture was toxic, disguised by perks that only made you feel like you had to stay longer at work, and the backstabbing and competitive environment was making me physically ill. My boyfriend reminded me that I cried literally all the time (I think I've blocked out those memories). I got UTIs from being too afraid to nip to the bathroom in between conference calls (I wouldn't wish this on my worst enemy).

So my savior—my only savior during these low moments at work—was going home and working on a project that I could do on my own laptop, from my own bed or couch, during TV commercial breaks or random free moments. It was heaven to be able to explore something different. The side hustle for me was something I enjoyed doing anyway, but I could faintly see a glimpse of opportunity in the future if I carried on doing it. Side hustles don't have to be financially orientated; in fact, it's better if they're not initially. That's why they are called side hustles: because your main hustle is what pays you for the most hours in the day.

A seesaw side hustle is something that allows you to stop and start a particular project. It doesn't take up all your time, and it can be resurrected as and when you need it. You might want to have a bunch of side projects going that can ebb and flow depending on how much work they are accumulating and how much time you have to give to them at that particular time.

PROS OF THE MULTI-HYPHEN LIFE

» Variety makes us happier and less bored. We are all more multifaceted than we think.

» Intense periods of energy on projects result in higher-quality work. It is exciting to work on something and give it everything you have with an end date in mind.

» Your overall brand of you is the umbrella for your multiple projects. An investment in your personal brand will make you stand out in the workplace.

» Productivity levels increase when you have some element of control over when you work.

» You can earn more money in a concentrated time period.

» You can embrace the idea of a nonlinear career (aka not climbing a premade ladder created by someone else).

» You are not labeled. You are not boxed in. You are not defined by one career.

» You are open to exploring your potential in multiple areas.

» You are more employable in future years because you have a variety of skills. You're less likely to be phased out. You are adaptable.

» You are future-proofing yourself. You are learning to twist and turn as you go.

» You can move quickly. In a big corporation, something as simple as designing a logo can take weeks; when you're a small business or by yourself, it can be done in a matter of hours. Getting time back is important, and being nimble is one of the most important things companies need to focus on right now.

CONS OF THE MULTI-HYPHEN LIFE

» It's a pain in the ass describing what you do to your grandparents.
» You have to set some serious boundaries. Work-life balance works only when you have some parameters in place.
» The character limit in your Twitter bio isn't enough to sum it all up.
» People will still want to put you into a box because it might make them uncomfortable that you don't have one clear job.
» You have to motivate yourself, which at times can be difficult to sustain.

Real-Life Multi-Hyphenates

Here are twelve case studies from a variety of different industries and career mixes, and here's how they make it work in individual ways.

ALYSSA, director of operations for a small independent publishing company, lead hostess at a local fine-dining Italian restaurant, social-media coordinator for several local businesses, and blogger

"I now wake up at 8 a.m. and write from 9 a.m. to 12:30 p.m. before making lunch and heading to work at the restaurant from 2 p.m. to 10 p.m. I still manage social-media accounts and do my best to schedule the content for these ahead of time, so as not to interrupt with my other work processes. Having multiple jobs makes me feel fulfilled! I feel like I've gained so many unique skills and find myself saying 'I can help with that!' when a friend or family member comes across a problem that they can't figure out. My favorite thing about my current lifestyle is that I feel accomplished at the end of each day. I may have old Gossip Girl episodes on the television in the background while I'm writing, but I'm ACTUALLY getting things done. Way more than I ever expected to be able to do in a single day. That's not to say that it's not hard. It's A LOT of work. But I've come to learn that nothing is going to come easy, and I'm happy to work for my future!"

OLIVIA, freelance copywriter-content designer-personal trainer

"I have this work setup by choice, after years of realizing what gets me up in the morning, what I'm good at, and what pays the bills. While I feel like I am making a positive impact through the power of my laptop—helping organizations who do some incredible things—the type of interaction from personal training is much more immediate and instantly gratifying. Switching between an email-centric, meeting-friendly freelancer to instructing a fitness class or a PT session challenges me to utilize both my personas on a regular basis. It means I don't get too complacent doing one thing for a long period of time."

HARRIET, founder of online gift box company-senior PR consultant-virtual assistant for a small yoga company

"I tend to do 75 percent for Nutkins Bakery, which consists of baking, packaging orders, posting them out, business admin, marketing, and PR. I then spend about 25 percent of my day doing freelance work, whether it's PR projects or as a virtual assistant answering emails and creating social content for a small yoga brand. It can be tiring spinning multiple plates, but most days I work from home, so it's much easier. One thing I would say is that organization is key. I plan out my week on a Sunday, and I always try to block out chunks of time for each project—without my bullet journal I wouldn't know whether I was coming or going. Having such different jobs certainly makes me feel creatively fulfilled, and it's also empowering knowing that I have control over the projects I'm working on and the type of work I'm accepting.

It makes me feel much more in control and independent than I did when I worked in the corporate world. I love that I can create my own days on my own time schedule, and if I need to change things around, I can. I quit my nine-to-five to have more freedom and to pursue a personal passion—having my fingers in multiple pies has allowed me to do that while also earning a living."

EMMA, senior pediatric clinical research nurse at a children's hospital-writer with a two-book deal

"I feel lucky to have opportunities in both nursing and writing, and I am pleased to be putting my education in both areas to good use. My job as a research nurse for children with rare diseases is fulfilling in the sense that I feel part of the driving force of change and innovation for treatment and medication. I also feel a sense of achievement as a soon-to-be published author. I like working in a clinical environment and having patient contact and then spending the evening in the company of publishers and writers and having entirely different experiences within a single day."

JAYNE, creative director-writer-social media manager-photo editor-illustrator[10]

"I've always been creative, and I've always promoted my work on the Internet, so I feel like I'm coming to a natural balance of roles now. I also like to have variety in my day, so these multiple job descriptions allow me to work on a mixture of projects, which keeps things interesting. This mixture of tasks keeps me fulfilled. I still don't know what the end result of my career will be in five, ten-plus years, but right now I like to be flexible with this, as you never know what opportunities might turn up in the future or what skills you might pick up and adore along the way."

ALI, HR product consultant-children's author

"I prioritize my consultancy work in terms of when I work. I usually agree to working days for the month and let the team know when I'm in the London office and when I'll be available but working remotely. If there's a need for me to be in the office on different days, I swap them around or do additional hours. The remainder of the week is managing the small design and development team I've brought together. Being able to swap heads, although a bit hectic and stressful at times, enables me to get much rounder job satisfaction."

ALLY, paramedic-blogger-photographer

"I'm currently working full-time with the ambulance service, so that takes up most of my time because I've been doing a lot of training but will be back to my normal schedule in the next few weeks, which means regular blocks of days off to fit in photography and blogging. On the occasions where the one job has taken over entirely, I've felt . . . well . . . unfulfilled is the perfect word for it. Eventually, I'd like to go part-time with the ambulance service and spend more time on my photography and blogging. But regardless I'd still want to carry on with all three."

VICTORIA, junior attorney-CEO of nonprofit Big Voice London

"I've always been the sort of person who prefers to be busy, so having multiple roles suits me well. Working in two different industries, particularly where they are slightly interconnected, is also a bonus. I know that I'm making the most of my time and my skills—both roles challenge me in different ways. I'm constantly learning during my training as a solicitor; I'm improving my legal advice, my approach to litigation, and my drafting. With my work at Big Voice London, I'm learning how to grow a charity, building relationships with sponsors, and leading a team of people. I have no doubt that doing both roles simultaneously is making me better at both jobs as a result."

ADAM, podcast producer-chef

"I was originally just a chef, but podcast production grew and grew. I began with one show and now produce two. I literally finish at the restaurant and go to work straight away on the podcasts. It was a choice, as I could have scaled back my podcasting ambitions, but now that I earn almost half my income from podcasting, I hope to grow it further and so am pouring my efforts into it. I always struggled to find the right creative outlet and for many years felt that I was merely existing to work. However, now that I have this creative outlet, I do feel as though I am achieving more with my life."

LOUISE, yoga teacher-life coach-PhD-nurse

"I am in charge of my own schedule. I can choose whatever days I want off and when to go on holidays. My PhD and life-coaching business and, additionally, writing my book mean I can work from anywhere. Currently, my regular weekly yoga classes and the odd nursing shifts I do keep me in London, but I could easily move and work abroad tomorrow if I wanted to. The idea that my earning potential is limitless is also another huge plus."

DONNA, marketing consultant-coach-event organizer

"I try to book a trip every few months, and going to the doctor's or the hairdresser's in the day is just a dream. I like being able to pop and see my dad for lunch if I finish early or pick my niece up from school. They are the moments that really matter in life, hey? And I love that midafternoon fresh air . . . I love getting involved in initiatives and projects for women, so I think that's where my work and life blend together. But when it comes to finishing work—I close my laptop, turn off my work phone, and close the door to my office. Home time is home time. The best piece of advice I could give is to calculate your monthly living costs, times that by three, and have that as your backup fund. I don't have a [retirement fund] at the moment, but I make sure I calculate how much tax I need to stash away each month, and I have a separate business account that all my invoices get paid to. That way, each month I just receive a salary like I would if I was employed."

Q&A with multi-hyphenate Clemency Burton-Hill, a radio and television broadcaster, author, journalist, musician, documentary maker, and live-events producer who also worked for a decade as a film and TV actress

In September 2018, after twenty-one years as a freelance multi-hyphenate, Clemency added her first "proper" job as creative director of music and arts at New York Public Radio, a role complete with a lanyard, business cards, and a corporate email address. She still juggles multiple side hustles including hosting two podcasts and live events, writing books, serving on the board of arts education charities, and consulting about music and the arts. She is on Twitter at @clemencybh.

Emma: Do you identify with being a multi-hyphenate?

Clemency: Absolutely. It's in my DNA. I am omnivorously curious and have always been instinctively drawn to playing across multiple platforms. I began juggling careers in my teens, when I played the violin very seriously, started acting professionally, and got my first freelance journalism gig. I am at my most creative, effective, and inspired when I have multiple mental browser tabs open and am working simultaneously on diverse projects. When I'm too focused on a single project, I genuinely start to panic!

Emma: Did you ever feel there was a stigma about having multiple interests?

Clemency: Yes—for years I would meet absolute bafflement from people when they asked what I did for a living, and I would constantly hear the refrain "But when are you going to make up your mind?" There was this underlying assumption, sometimes even articulated outright to me, that I couldn't be serious about anything if I wasn't focused—that whole "jack-of-all-trades, master of none" thing. I graduated in 2003, back when "portfolio careers" were seen as some sort of joke, and of course nobody had ever heard of the Multi-

Hyphen Life, whose ethos I was living day by day. (Sometimes when people asked me what I did, I would reply, "I'm a juggler," resulting in some odd looks and one person even replying, appalled, "What, in a circus?") I felt for a long time as though I wasn't taken seriously: that people viewed me as some kind of unhinged, indecisive dilettante. I didn't let that stop me, as I knew the only way to answer those criticisms was simply to get on with producing excellent work, my way, but it was tough sometimes.

Emma: What do you think the positives of this lifestyle are?

Clemency: Of course, there is the enormously liberating freedom of being your own boss, able to control your own workflow, explore your genuine curiosities, and (theoretically) only take on projects you truly care about. But for me, above all else, the most positive aspect of the Multi-Hyphen Life is the intellectual and emotional reward I get from combining so many different parts of my brain in different ways and feeling the crackle of unexpected connections when projects collide and cross-pollinate. If you look at my résumé, on paper sometimes it doesn't make sense, but I can't tell you how often that unexpected connection happens. I believe nothing is wasted experience: Everything is connected.

Emma: Are there any negatives in your opinion?

Clemency: Financial insecurity and professional lack of clarity—people "in charge" seemingly not taking you seriously because you can't easily answer the question "What do you do?" Also, it depends on the gig: One day something that seems super positive—like being your own boss, self-directing your own workflow—can feel somewhat negative the next because maybe you actually feel like working with a team that day or you'd appreciate some feedback or support from others. It can be lonely and occasionally isolating to work like this, so it's vital to find your own support network, team, or colleagues. Also, time management can be challenging: Personally, I am terrible at creating boundaries and have never yet managed to nail the work-life balance. There is no such thing as work vs. life for me: I work literally all the time, and that's not necessarily healthy—I know.

Emma: What things do you wish you'd known before?

Clemency: As a kind of "grandmother" millennial, born in the early 1980s, who didn't even get an email address until I was eighteen, I felt incredibly out on a limb for many early years of my career. I felt nobody really got what I was doing. I wish I'd known that the world was actually on the cusp of this seismic change, one in which technology was about to disrupt everything and in which the way I was instinctively carving out my career would come to be seen as not only not-freakish but actually desirable, even smart. In other words, I wish there had been The Multi-Hyphen Life and all its attendant support, wisdom, and advice back when I was breaking into the workforce. It might have led to fewer sleepless nights along the way!

I loved hearing these stories, especially how different some of the mixes are and how they make it work. These accounts hammer home that there is no one-size-fits-all solution nor one answer; it's a personal and individual setup, but there are lots and lots of people who are making it work and mixing and matching their careers. And you can do it too. Keep reading for more practical examples and tips in the coming chapters on blending work and home, avoiding burnout, money, and the tool kit (chapter 7).

Chapter 4

OUR NEW WORK SELF

"We subscribe to the belief that women contain multitudes and that all of those parts need to be nurtured and appreciated."

—AUDREY GELMAN, co-founder of The Wing[1]

One of the most frequently asked questions I get is along the lines of: "If I was going to lead a multi-hyphenate lifestyle, what impact would that have on my sense of self or identity?" Because, let's face it, a lot of us hide behind a fancy job title because it makes us feel good. But with many jobs dissolving and becoming irrelevant in a new world of work, our career identities are no longer terribly stable anyway. I get asked how to go about introducing yourself or explaining what you do in social or networking situations. (You'll find more on the practicalities of networking in chapter 9.) It's a good question, because you don't technically have just one main job, so what do you do? How can you feel the same amount of external validation from having a big, impressive job title to fall back on? When discussing the pros and cons of being a multi-hyphenate, it crops up time and time again as a concern. Perhaps you are worried that your work identity might feel weaker if you are not married to one company. A lot of who we are is tied up in our workplace roles whether we like it or not. It's clear that our work is connected to how we perceive ourselves and our purpose in the world—be it in a practical or more spiritual sense.

What Do You Do?

When did our identities get so wrapped up in work? It makes sense that we place so much importance on it—we spend most of our waking hours at work and in the company of colleagues, so of course it shapes us. But I argue that leading a multi-hyphenate lifestyle helps you have a more fully realized identity; it allows you to explore and express all areas of your personality. You can have a more rounded identity because you are reaching into hidden corners and introducing yourself as a complete person, not as a floating job title. It paves the way for more authentic connections, too.

This fear of how we explain our job is a result of just how much we care about how others perceive us and our sound-bite culture. We need to sell ourselves in tweets, have a sharp LinkedIn bio, write a catchy email subject. Anything that takes too long to explain may have no listeners left at the end. We want a strong elevator pitch, and we don't have any time to waste. Having a few different hyphens on your résumé means you can't necessarily sum up what you do very quickly or easily. It can take time, or you might have to choose which hat to lead with. It takes strategy to know which bits of your bio are specifically relevant in certain situations. Being a multi-hyphenate means you are less fully attached to one sole career identity and, therefore, there's less riding on how you come across when describing your job. Yes, you are less easily identified, summed up, or placed in a neat box, but that's OK.

Work up your own elevator pitch that succinctly sums up what you do, drawing in links between the hyphens (see below). It helps to come up with umbrella terms to sum things up. For me, I say that I'm an author and broadcaster. Under "author" I can list writing books, magazine articles, and blog posts, and "broadcaster" houses radio, podcasting, and TV work. Loads of hyphens but described under only two job career roofs.

TIPS FOR WRITING YOUR ELEVATOR PITCH:

1. Write down what you do, including all the hyphens.
   Example: At the moment, I'm doing "x," but I'm also working on "y."
2. Come up with an overarching mission statement that applies to everything you do.
   Example: On the whole, my mission is to . . .
3. Speak more about why you love or do what you do (people like to hear the why in career scenarios).
   Example: I love these jobs/this mixture of careers because . . . and it allows me to do . . .

Since the launch of social media and designing our own online profiles, we now have an online personality whether we like it or not. When people scoff at the idea of having a personal brand, they might not be aware that even by simply having a public Facebook or Instagram page, you are essentially a brand. You have a bio, a profile picture, a mission, and content. We have many different sides to us online: multiple seemingly contradictory interests, many different opinions, we tweet from the sofa at home, we answer online polls, we share our political beliefs in a Facebook status and project our hopes and dreams on our blogs or Pinterest feeds. We are publishers of our own corners of the Internet. Yes, our digital footprint might be scrutinized occasionally, but mostly we are simply curating our own online worlds.

In this Twitter bio culture, it matters how quickly we make an impression online, in our photos, bios, and words. We have more and more competition for people's time, attention, and eyeballs on something. According to researchers at the Missouri University of Science and Technology, "It takes less than two-tenths of a second for an online visitor to form a first opinion of your brand once they've perused your company's website. And it takes just another 2.6 seconds for that viewer's eyes to concentrate in a way that reinforces that first impression."[2]

I used to feel like I had to be or sound impressive the minute I walked into a room and, otherwise, I wasn't succeeding. It was a shock how important that had been to me when I quit my job at Condé Nast. I used to be able to walk into a room and introduce myself, and people would be immediately impressed because they could place me with a big household media name and this made it easier to mingle. But now I prefer the challenge of truly connecting with people on my own merits, using my elevator pitch to sell myself and my work.

Even though I am happier and richer (in all senses of the word), it is harder to sum up what I do and to give people an immediate context to my work. It means I don't have an easy, lazy way out. I don't cut corners when I introduce myself and expect people to know what I do. Instead, I have to talk about my different work interests and hobbies, and it doesn't matter whether people don't find them impressive. The main thing is that I enjoy them and I make money from them—our hyphens are a personal relationship that we have with the world and what we do.

In an interview in the *Atlantic*, Miya Tokumitsu, the author of *Do What You Love: And Other Lies about Success and Happiness*, said, "I've tried this little experiment when I meet people in non-work situations and try to see how long I can talk to them without asking about their work or have them ask me about my work. It's actually really hard to last longer than four minutes." But having multiple hyphens allows you to have a bit of distance between your job and who you are. You are a mixture of things. We are all much more than just our job title.

I was thinking about how social media has perhaps made us braver and more open when it comes to being ourselves. In some ways our phones know more intimate details about us than our partners do. When it comes to the workplace, I think our thoughts, opinions, interests, and personality traits matter more than ever. We are now more able to present our full selves.

It's Not Just About Branding Yourself but Rebranding Yourself as You Go

There are dangers of becoming too attached to your Internet self. You might end up spending too much time online because you like how your online self makes you feel and appear to the world. And in most jobs now (and in our leisure time) we do spend a disproportionate amount of time online. It's hard not to. However, the benefits usually outweigh the dangers, particularly when it comes to work. You can make something a reality online that IRL would be tricky (opening a shop, getting funding, creating a product, finding an audience in order to sell something niche). A company that has started to descend in popularity and profit can get a new lease on life online with a shiny new website, digital marketing campaign, PR, or supporters with an online following. According to *Business Today*, Starbucks "pulled itself out of the financial meltdown of 2008 by aligning its operations with customer demands through social media." They launched a multilingual Facebook page to deal with customer service issues across all platforms and offer recipes and tips on their popular YouTube channel. LEGO came close to financial collapse in 2003–2004 and were revived by big social-media collaborations and film franchises; they are now thriving. The Help Refugees charity started with just one hashtag, #HelpCalais, used by a few people. This hashtag has now grown into a million-pound, legitimate nonprofit in just a couple of years.

The same methods can help a person who wants to start a new career. Think about exploring different platforms that might elevate you. The Internet allows you to sell yourself and your products in whatever way you want to. Tech has allowed anyone to put whatever they want into the world. It is possible to get noticed from any small seed online.

In *Selfie: How We Became So Self-Obsessed and What It's Doing to Us*, author Will Storr writes about "the blank slate view," or the idea that anyone can achieve anything: "It is instinctively, addictively attractive to people because we want to believe that anyone can achieve anything.

It's a lovely story, and it's one our culture tells us repeatedly. But it's not true."[3] Of course, it's not true that everyone has the same start in life or the exact same opportunities. Some people are better placed—privileged in race, class, or education, for example—than others to succeed. But there have been some improvements. Decades ago, getting into a competitive industry really was impossible without knowing someone or having an "in." However, I do think that in this Internet age it is easier to break through traditional barriers. Our voices can rise up to the top more easily. We have the best possible chance, at least. The old gatekeepers are slowly disappearing. Before social media, before this age where everyone can connect with anyone at the click of a button, it really did matter whom you knew. The world is still full of huge inequalities, but I do believe that tech has allowed more people to get their own foot in the door. I hope this continues.

Having a Whole Sense of Self Matters

Being a multi-hyphenate allows me to feel as though I am being myself. I feel like I don't have that much of a separation between work and play because I am merging myself across the two. Everyone has multiple facets to their personalities, and all those different selves have different needs. A multi-hyphenate career nurtures and nourishes these selves and brings out our best skills and abilities.

You might cringe at the idea of someone knowing the real you at work, because you'd rather get your stuff done and leave. I used to be that person, too, and when my boss (female) used to quiz me on my dating life during a meeting, I wanted to curl up and disappear into another dimension like in *Stranger Things*. When it comes to the self in relation to work, who we are and what we believe have a huge part to play, in and out of the office. I think we should encourage everyone to be more themselves at work. By being yourself, you might find that parts of your personality—like being opinionated, being active, or being a good public speaker—would benefit your role at work.

Social media lets us merge our work and personal selves online. The Internet has allowed us to express so many different sides of ourselves: our hobbies, kids, pets, interests, career choices. It can offer a holistic perspective of our own lives. We, in turn, can use these tools to learn about our colleagues' lives. It can be a bit like seeing your teacher outside of school and thinking, *Oh my God, you're actually a person who does person things*. It's difficult to keep a hard separation now, even if we wanted to.

There's a notion that's been growing in popularity: "Bring your whole self to work." Mike Robbins did a 2015 TEDx talk with this exact title. In his talk, Mike said:

> For organizations, particularly in the twenty-first century, what it really takes for us to be fulfilled and successful is an ability to bring our whole selves to work. All of who we are. All the gifts, all the talents, the fears, the doubts, the insecurities, the things that matter most. But what that involves for us as individuals and organizations of various sizes is actually a lot of courage.

Bringing your whole self to work means not hiding away from awkward conversations. It means having human-to-human conversations about when life gets in the way and having real conversations with colleagues about things. It means allowing my different interests and facets of my personality to show. I've found in my multi-hyphenate career that I've finally been able to bring my whole self to my job. The multiple sides of my personality come out and offer different skills in different situations, with different people.

Being Our Real Selves at Work Is Very Important

We are often afraid of being unique, standing out, or upsetting the status quo. We think that hiding away our real selves might help us blend in and get ahead, but, in fact, we need to be more ourselves. But in their paper for Deloitte titled "Uncovering Talent: A New Model of Inclusion" Kenji Yoshino at NYU School of Law and Christie Smith, managing principal, Deloitte University Leadership Center for Inclusion, found that allowing and encouraging people to be their real selves at work have many benefits, including helping companies achieve more diversity.

Not being our true selves at work means we are not as able to bond with our colleagues because we are giving only half of ourselves away. It means we need to work harder to get a boss or colleague to buy in because they know only half the story.

Hiding parts of ourselves and our identity is not just about personality either; it can be an attempt to subvert prejudice and stigma in the workplace. According to Yoshino and Smith, "29% of respondents said they hide aspects of their appearance. Women reported wearing clothes that are more masculine because they feel their colleagues will be more likely to take them seriously."[4] But bringing more aspects of ourselves into the workplace can improve our working life and enable us to make stronger bonds with colleagues and clients. It's about exploring different aspects of ourselves that showcase what we could bring to work and hopefully means we are seen in a more open-minded way.

Leading the multi-hyphenate life encourages complexity and multitudes. You are allowed to embrace all sides of yourself, you don't have to hide anything because you are functioning in a way that suits you, and you can be your full self with no exceptions and reap the benefits of improved overall well-being and productivity levels. Hiding ourselves or pretending to be someone else is not beneficial to the company or to ourselves in the long run.

Personal Branding Isn't New

You may think the phrase "personal branding" is an irritating new buzzword, but personal branding is not new at all. It's been important for decades, centuries even. Your name is your brand, and what you do that is specifically you is the reason people pick you for the job. Who you are has always mattered, but in the age of social media it matters so much more. Your Google results are your résumé. Your Twitter bio is your elevator pitch. Your website is your shop window. Everything about you online can help sell who you are. You have a brand even if you've never been on the Internet in your life—but if you are going to play the Internet game, you need to work on a strong brand identity for you and your work.

According to Cecile Alper Leroux, vice president of HCM innovation at Ultimate Software: "through conversations with our customers, as well as media coverage, [we observed] that something was happening in the world regarding the way people identify themselves in relation to their employment. Where someone works is much less relevant to employees' identities."[5] Less importance is placed on our job to tell the story of who we are, and I think that is a positive thing. It means we can avoid jobs that look good on paper but might not be right for us and instead choose jobs because we feel that they suit us. We have more freedom now, to explore lots of different avenues, to try out different sides of our personality. "Rebranding" the "personal brand" to encompass your whole self is a great way to update an old concept for today. We are humans, not brands.

THREE TIPS ON BRANDING YOUR PERSONAL ONLINE SPACE:

1. Be visible: It's important when building a brand to be visible consistently over time. Make sure you are regularly posting at a time where people can see you. This will differ from person to person, but you can use a tool like Iconosquare to help you find your best times to post. Quality over quantity is important, but repetition of what works is key.

2. Have a strong USP (unique selling point): Like any brand, pinpoint what makes you different. Stand out from your peers. Dig into the real reason you are doing what you're doing. Paul

Arden's book *Whatever You Think, Think the Opposite* is a good guide here. Pinpointing the opposite of your initial responses is a good exercise to challenge yourself and your first instincts. We're often naturally trend followers, so it's good to brainstorm ideas that go against the norms.

3. Collaborate: Work with and alongside people you admire, who share the same ethics and values as you. The people you choose to work with reflect on you and your brand.

THE REASONS PERSONAL BRANDING IS HERE TO STAY:

1. We live in an increasingly visual world: It's important that people can easily distinguish the look and feel of your work in a sea of other competitors.

2. Online profiles are evolving: We might change social platforms in the future, but our personal brand will evolve and live on over time. Our brand will remain, even when platforms or apps change.

3. Online recruitment will only grow in the future: Many companies already recruit solely using online searches on candidates, so being in control of your online brand is really crucial to how you attract new work.

4. Personal brands can help build genuine connections: With a strong, real online brand, people can understand you, your intentions, your motivations, and your work in a matter of seconds. It means we can connect with like-minded people or search out the right people for a project or the best new hire for a team more easily.

Building a personal brand is not a vanity project. It's not about building your Instagram following or even about looking good. It's about talent retention. Job security is scarce, there are fewer barriers to entry for most jobs, and competition is fierce. Before the Internet, your company couldn't recruit from a global pool of people. Things have changed. As *New York Times* columnist Tom Friedman put it: "If you have a challenge that's posed to you, why in the world would you limit yourself simply to the talent within your own company? Because the odds of it being the best in this world are really pretty low."[6] Companies can now recruit contractors and experts and hire them on specific projects. Employing workers full-time might not make sense in the future as companies change and grow so quickly. They may be more likely to recruit externally and see who the best people are on a case-by-case basis. This, of course, sounds scary, but you can prepare for it.

Personal branding can help you in your multi-hyphenate career because it helps you easily explain who you are and what you do to the increasing number of people in your network. In the future when the majority of people are contractors and solo workers and when companies outsource more than hire full-time, you will want to stand out, whether your skills are niche or very broad or a combination. It's not whom you know but who knows you.

The Art of Self-Promoting Without Selling Your Soul

With the rise of the online entrepreneur, self-promotion has become a new normal. Doing an Instagram story directing people to our newest project is commonplace. But is this work, or is this play? As a society, we are now rewarded for being seen. Likes, comments, followers—they turn into something tangible. Followers can turn into money, whether it's eyeballs on our work leading to more work, free clothes, sponsorships, or other perks. Our following has value. We are social animals who enjoy being seen and feeling like we matter. We aren't necessarily to blame if we feel we must self-promote to get ahead, especially if we have tangible results at the end of it. You simply cannot get more work without promoting yourself. You are a business, and you need to market yourself in any way you can. However, there's of course a difference between bragging and promoting. Highlighting your work is not the same as bragging, which will leave you with no one left to promote to!

TIPS FOR SELF-PROMOTING WITHOUT FEELING ICKY:

» **Ask yourself why:** Make sure people know why you are promoting the thing you are promoting. Is it because you're proud, happy, worried, wanting something specific, or even openly needing the money? Being open about your motivations makes the promoting feel more human.

» **Make something you like or would be interested in yourself:** Make sure you're proud of what you are sharing. This seems obvious, but if you make/build/launch something that you like, promoting it will feel natural, and you'll be excited to share it, not embarrassed.

» **Use your voice:** The most distinctive way of promoting your work is by speaking in your own voice. Write in a way that feels as close to your speaking voice as possible. Forcing yourself to be overly "authentic" can end up feeling just as false as "salespeak." It's best to imagine you are speaking to people IRL and telling them in a conversational way about what you're doing.

» **Don't be too harsh on yourself:** You'd probably tell a friend to go for it or not overthink it or be less judgmental, so try to apply that to yourself. It's not the end of the world if something doesn't resonate; you can try something different tomorrow. Take small risks with the way you promote yourself. It's OK to fail.

» **Talk to the right people:** Self-promotion hardly ever feels icky if you are talking to an audience that wants to hear from you. Email newsletters are a great way to build a connected audience because it's a group of people who have opted in. It feels less like you are broadcasting to an empty or busy room.

Why You Should Add a Self-Care Hyphen to Your Job Title

What if adding an extra hyphen to your life isn't actually about work at all? In her book *The Self-Care Project*, Jayne Hardy wrote about how self-care can help revive you during mental health dips:

"I missed writing—it was something I'd always loved until depression sapped the joy and self-belief out of it for me. I decided that writing a beauty blog might help me with self-care. To write about beauty products I'd have to use beauty products—self-care right there! That little blog helped me in ways I'm not sure I can properly put into words; it gave me purpose, distracted me from the suicidal thoughts, injected pleasure back into writing, brought sunshine back into my life."

Adding personal hyphens into your life can definitely be an act of self-care. Having a side hustle is often a business venture, but it doesn't always have to be. I have felt that having side projects makes me feel creative when many jobs didn't. They allowed me to escape into something that is just mine and that I had total control over. Self-care can come in many forms, and all that matters is that you are doing something that is purely for yourself and your own mental health or relaxation. This looks different for all of us, but allowing yourself time for something that sits outside of work and home to-do lists feels quite empowering and nourishing for the mind and soul.

Regularly doing something that we enjoy isn't selfish or self-indulgent; it's actually crucial to our well-being. Tom Rath and Jim Harter's PhD paper published by UCL, "Your Career Well-Being and Your Identity," describes well-being: "At a fundamental level, we all need something to do, and ideally something to look forward to, when we wake up every day." When it comes to our careers, having something enjoyable on the side can really make a positive difference: "If you don't have the opportunity to regularly do something you enjoy—even if it's more of a passion or interest than something you get paid to do—the odds of you having high well-being in other areas diminish rapidly."

The *New York Times* recently published a feature on burnout, a term we all know too well (and there is a whole chapter on it to follow), especially in today's working world where we can easily work 24-7 if we're not careful. The article stated that one of the ways to combat burnout is by having "a hobby outside of work through which you can decompress, de-stress and dissociate from work."[7] Finding something to turn to that relaxes you is important and doesn't need to have a bigger agenda beyond that.

Self-care is much more than buying a few material things every now and again. The *hygge* trend (the Danish ritual of enjoying life's simple pleasures) got some backlash when it turned into a huge moneymaker. Buying an expensive candle or faux-fur rug became a stand-in for real self-care. Of course, truly taking care of yourself goes deeper than a Body Shop splurge. We have to make sure that self-care runs into the crevices of our lifestyles, making us able to function better and giving us time to realize we matter, that our brain and body matter, and that we need to make time for ourselves alongside of work.

In one study, research scientist Zorana Ivcevic Pringle found that people who engaged in everyday forms of creativity such as taking photographs, making collages, or writing for pleasure tended to be more open-minded, curious, positive, energetic, and motivated by their activity. These activities also led to increased feelings of well-being and personal satisfaction compared with fellow classmates who were less engaged in everyday creativity.[8] A 2018 study in the United Kingdom found that doctors prescribing arts activities to their patients resulted in a significant drop in hospital admissions.[9]

Having a hyphen that allows you to be more creative, open up more, and exercise those muscles you don't use in other aspects of your life could be life changing. Having something that you do that makes you feel more like the best version of yourself can increase your confidence and open more doors for you.

Chapter 5

BURNOUT CULTURE

Can I admit something to you? I love Urban Dictionary. I often prefer its definitions and colloquial language over standard dictionaries. It feels more real (and funny and, obviously, occasionally very rude). When I typed in "burnout," it came up with this:

> A state of emotional and physical exhaustion caused by a prolonged period of stress and frustration; an inevitable corporate condition characterized by frequent displays of unprofessional behavior, a blithe refusal to do any work, and most important, a distinct aura of not giving a shit.

This is also how I define and detect burnout when it comes to my own behavior. If I have lost interest, find myself canceling exciting meetings because of anxiety, get snappy with my colleagues and friends, or have a glazed-over aura of not caring about my career, I know burnout is upon me. I know that I need to seriously change my ways, take a step back, and prioritize and protect my mental health. And take some sort of action.

Of course, I should include the official definition of burnout too. According to psychologist David Ballard, PsyD, MBA: "Burn-out can be defined as 'an extended period of time where someone experiences exhaustion and a lack of interest in things.'"[1]

I haven't always been a multi-hyphenate waving the flag for
flexibility. I worked in a rigid, nonflexible structure for years because
I didn't know there was any other option. There's a lack of knowledge
about what different jobs are out there and that flexibility is available.
(And another part of the problem is still a lingering stigma when
it comes to anyone who works in a way different from the norm.)
According to a 2017 report from Timewise, there are "8.7 million
people who don't currently work flexibly, but would like to if the jobs
were there." In my fast-paced job working for a top media company,
I started to realize how ill I was getting as a result of the long hours
and the stress of relentlessly demanding bosses. I had an old boss
who shouted "YOU CAN SLEEP WHEN YOU'RE DEAD" at
me whenever I complained about being a bit overworked. I was so
stressed in one job that I started getting nocturnal anxiety (yes, going
to the toilet about eighteen times a night is not normal for a twenty-
something). I went to the doctor, and my bladder was fine—it was the
anxiety. Then there were the recurring UTIs from feeling like I had
to work through normal bathroom breaks. These are two extreme
examples, but the physical toll of our stresses can go unnoticed for
months or even years. It's no surprise that burnout is on the rise. We
are in the midst of combating our fears of becoming irrelevant in a
world that is changing rapidly. In general, we fear change. We fear
changing our lives and the model that has existed forever. People fear
that changing their careers means starting all over again. But the pace
of work is changing, and moving to a new job doesn't necessarily mean
going backward or having to study and retrain. A lot of the new digital
jobs simply require getting your hands dirty.

We are more anxious than ever. A report from
PricewaterhouseCoopers found: "More than a third of the UK
workforce is experiencing anxiety, depression, or stress, according to
a survey of employees in junior and senior roles." The study also says
that of those employees who have taken time off due to the stress and
anxiety: "39 percent said they did not feel comfortable telling their

employer about the issue."[2] We might be talking about it to our friends in the pub or in anonymous forums, but we don't seem to be openly discussing it in the workplace. We are oversharing in other ways: tweeting what we had for breakfast, blogging about our sex lives, and sharing our temporary profile pictures on Facebook that show which political party we vote for. But it seems that our relationship with our work and the anxieties it can present are still quite difficult subjects.

While Instagram presents a rosy take on life, in conversations with my friends in private WhatsApp groups, we are open about our anxieties and fears. Our truth comes out in what Alexis C. Madrigal coined as "dark social," which is the various forms of private messaging we engage in. Relatedly, "dark traffic" is described as "the result of people sharing website links through email, text messages, and private chats." So the conversation is happening, and the links are being shared—but mostly in private messaging—so we can't always see it. What we see on public profiles is a very small piece of the pie.

Fears of redundancy, fears of not working hard enough, fears of working too hard and heading toward burnout, fears of moving into the freelance life, and fears of not having the courage to move jobs or start a side hustle—It seems we are in need of guidance and no holds-barred honesty about how to cultivate a healthy work-life balance. Some of us live to work; some work to live. But there is one thing we have in common, and that's how plugged in we all are now. I'm particularly interested in how we can try to make technology work for us, not against us, in allowing us to have more freedom and to be less burned out and stressed.

The Multi-Hyphen Life is not about working long hours. It's about short, productive bursts. More breaks, more bursts of energy. It's a different way of working. This, of course, goes against the many assumptions about multi-hyphenates: that we are workaholics who burn ourselves out by working all week and then working a side gig on the weekend. In the United States, the General Social Survey, a nationwide survey that since 1972 has tracked the attitudes and behaviors of

American society, found that in 2016, 50 percent of respondents were consistently exhausted because of work, compared with 18 percent two decades earlier.[3] Is tech to blame? Possibly. There's no denying it's improved our productivity in countless ways, but are we in dire need of boundaries? Do we need our employers to lead by example? I think so.

According to Eastern Kentucky University, companies spend $300 billion annually for healthcare and missed work days as a result of workplace stress.[4] That's what happens when you push and push and keep asking for more from people inside a rigid structure. Asking for flexible working hours can change the way we work and the limits we set on ourselves. The work will get done, but in less restrictive circumstances. We must trust employees to get their work done in their own way. Nathaniel Kleitman, a groundbreaking physiologist and sleep researcher, wrote that our brains can focus on any given task for only 90 to 120 minutes at a time. Since I came across that research, I section off my time in spurts. I don't think, *What can I get done in this entire day*? Instead, I think, *What can I achieve in ninety-minute sessions with breaks in between*? I work fewer hours than my pre-multi-hyphenate days and get more done because I do it at times of my own peak productivity. Some days I will get more done in one ninety-minute burst than I do if I work a whole day nonstop.

Technology has blurred the lines between work and play more than ever, and it's opened up brand-new conversations about their relationship, both good (flexibility!) and bad (burnout). A 2018 feature in the *Guardian* found that "technology was supposed to liberate us from much of the daily slog but has often made things worse: in 2002, fewer than 10% of employees checked their work email outside of office hours. Today, with the help of tablets and smartphones, it is 50%, often before we get out of bed."[5]

We need to start having these sorts of conversations openly with friends and colleagues, and it's important, now more than ever, to admit we are overwhelmed. It's also important that we're not afraid to admit, "I don't know where I'm going in my career" or "I feel like

I'm wasting time online." It's OK to feel confused right now, but it's time to take matters into your own hands if you are feeling jaded or let down. It's not about turning your back on traditional employment, but it is about doing your own thing on the side and wrapping a layer of empowerment and protection around yourself in an unstable job market. At a time of vulnerability, we need to use the tools we have and do the best we can. But we also need to learn what our own personal boundaries and limits are while doing so. What tips us over the edge? How much can we do without starting to go downhill? What does balance actually look like to each of us? Has the limit of what we can cope with changed?

Burnout is real. Technology still sometimes feels like an exciting feast that we want to binge on. It's here, and it's all around us. But most of us are on the edge of burnout or have experienced it at some point or watched a friend suffer because of it. We push and push, deplete our internal resources, and hit zero. You hit negative figures. Burnout takes over until we figure out a way to get more in the tank again.

HOW TO SPOT BURNOUT
» Feeling really cynical about everyone and everything
» Becoming more apathetic than usual; not caring that much about the outcome of your work
» Tasks that were once quite easy become difficult or overwhelming.
» Physical symptoms like recurring illnesses, weak immune system, aches, or pains
» Isolating yourself
» Feeling a huge loss of energy

HOW TO AVOID BURNOUT IF YOU SPOT TELLTALE SIGNS
» Prioritize your sleep (and I recommend curling up with the book *Why We Sleep* by Matthew Walker).
» Start saying no more often, however difficult that might be.

» Cancel any plans that are making you feel anxious.

» Focus on important aspects of a to-do list and don't overwork yourself on "nice-to-haves."

» Practice self-care, whether that's getting more fresh air and alone time or doing a creative hobby that relaxes you.

» Take a step back and write down the things that are stressing you out. Bullet journals can help with this exercise.

» Lie in bed for a few minutes each morning without immediately checking your phone.

» Try to break up overwhelming tasks into small, bite-size chunks.

It's Time to Get Rid of Sleep Stigma

We can't help it, but we often judge people who prioritize sleep. Someone recently said to me: "We don't call babies lazy when they sleep all the time; they are growing!" Sleep is so important. According to the US National Heart, Lung, and Blood Institute (NHLBI), "Sleep deficiency can lead to physical and mental health problems, injuries, loss of productivity, and even a greater risk of death." So why do we still think we don't need much of it and that work can encroach on this precious commodity?

I am personally a big fan of naps. Sometimes when I admit this, I feel like I might be judged for it because we appear culturally allergic to sleeping. Naps are normally thought of as for the lazy and unambitious. But I've found there have been so many benefits to napping when it comes to my life and work. I feel more refreshed after one and find I can work longer. I feel more in control of my life and schedule. It helps break up the day. Scientists have shown that a sixty- to ninety-minute siesta can charge up our brain's batteries as much as eight hours tucked up in bed.[6]

In Madrid, Spain, nap classes have popped up at spas and gyms, and a nap bar has opened called Siesta & Go (what a great name). On arrival, you can choose from a menu of options in either private or shared rooms. Naps can be booked by the minute or hour, costing between $8 (one hour in a bunk) and $14 (an hour in a segregated room). You can book or walk in off the street. Genius. Of course, in Spain, it is culturally the norm to nap in the afternoon, but imagine if this were available for everyone, everywhere!

More than 85 percent of mammalian species are what's called "polyphasic sleepers," which means they sleep for short bursts throughout the day instead of in one block like humans do, suggesting that our sleep routine isn't in keeping with other mammals.[7] Eleanor Roosevelt, Winston Churchill, Leonardo da Vinci, and Albert Einstein are all famous nappers.[8]

In his book *Why We Sleep*, Matthew Walker calls people who boast about not sleeping the "sleepless elite." In a piece in *Business Insider*, he said, "Sleep deprivation depletes stores of your 'natural killer cells,' a type of lymphocyte (white blood cell) that nix tumor and virus cells. A single 4- or 5-hour night of sleep could lower your body's 'natural killer' cell count by around 70%."[9] Lack of sleep is literally killing us.

Tech also affects our sleep patterns. According to sleep.org, about 72 percent of children age six to seventeen sleep with at least one electronic device in their bedroom. The blue light from our phones suppresses melatonin production, keeping our brains alert, and phones' lights, vibrations, and sounds can keep waking us up throughout the night. Knowing how important sleep is to our overall well-being, it's no surprise "sleep hygiene"—including reducing our use of tech before bed—has become more popular. Prioritizing healthy sleep habits is essential to avoiding burnout.

Hobbies Are Not the Same as Side Hustles

Burnout can rear its ugly head when we're overstretching ourselves. One thing to keep in mind is that not everything should turn into a moneymaking, scheming side hustle. Some things should be kept sacred and purely for leisure. Enjoying something does not mean you should try to turn it into a business venture. If you are someone who loves taking baths, it doesn't mean you *need* to launch a side hustle selling bath products online. I mean, you could, but you might also just love taking baths as part of your much-needed leisure time. Be mindful of the difference. Protect your hobbies.

How Job Sharing Can Free You Up and Broaden Your Horizons

Let's talk for a moment about job sharing. This setup can allow you to work flexibly in a role while allowing you to cultivate your other hyphens outside of the office. In a former workplace of mine, two editors at our magazine shared a job. One worked Monday and Tuesday, the other Wednesday, Thursday, Friday. They shared their work via email and in phone calls. They made it as seamless as possible and had each other's backs. I observed their system and was in awe of the way they made it work. The work always got done, and it was done really well. In a job share your boss is winning too; they technically get two brains for the price of one. Yes, these editors got half the wages, but in their days off they pursued other work or hobbies that fulfilled them in different ways and were other possible streams of income. Job sharing allowed them to keep their options open, meet new contacts, and make extra money, all while holding down a day job that covered their bills and didn't make them tear their hair out.

I interviewed Lindsay Frankel, a journalist at the *Times* (UK) and a former colleague of mine. Lindsay also job shared in the same office as me, and it looked like it was working for her. I found it really inspiring when I discovered that Lindsay had actively put herself forward for job sharing. I asked how she was able to ask for this setup, as it's still not seen as the "norm." She responded: "I didn't ever think it was an option for me, as I don't have children . . . It was the editor offering it up who made me consider I could be eligible. And once I got the job, it opened my eyes to the fact that I could be more available to my elderly mum or just spend better time with my niece and nephew (like picking them up from school on a Monday because I didn't have to race back to London after a weekend visiting). Just not work all the time like I had done for the past twenty years. It's not just parents who benefit from flexibility."

As someone currently without children, I often felt judged for wanting flexibility and a multi-hyphenate career with days "off." I asked her whether she had any advice on making a job share work for those who might be considering it. Lindsay said: "Don't be competitive. I think this is vital. I didn't want the whole job; neither did she. I didn't try to be her and vice versa. I think this meant we could trust each other. I can't imagine job sharing with someone you thought was trying to shaft you!"

HOW TO MAKE JOB SHARING WORK

After interviewing Lindsay and speaking to others who successfully job share, here is a pie chart presenting my take on what's required for this setup to work, to be taken as a loose starting point.

What's required for successful job sharing

93

Glorifying "Busy" Is Bad for Us

Long hours without breaks mean we run out of energy and concentration. We know we can't work solidly for long periods of time, and yet we push through and try to do just that. Talking to friends of mine who are lawyers and doctors, it is clear that overwork leads to resentment and mistakes and lost productivity. The Japanese have a word for "death by overworking": *karōshi*. The major medical causes of *karōshi* deaths are heart attacks and strokes due to stress and starvation. This phenomenon is also widespread in South Korea, where it is referred to as *gwarosa*. In China, overwork-induced death is called *guolaosi*. Just because we can do more doesn't mean we should.

Consultant Cali Williams Yost wrote: "Working harder and faster in the hopes of staying safe can be counterproductive. You neglect your health. You don't sleep or eat well. You don't exercise or take a vacation to recharge. You don't nurture your professional network or your personal support system. But your boss can't tell you when to focus on the parts of life that keep you healthy and happy."[10]

The metric of success used to be "busy." It still is, in some ways. Kudos often go to the workers who look like they are the busiest. I worked in this sort of environment for years. We feel as though every single moment of time needs to be filled to the brim in order to get the most out of every second of every day—and reap the reputational rewards that come with it.

Being busy is still something that people like to brag about. Yahoo's Marissa Mayer told Bloomberg News that she used to work 130-hour workweeks.[11] Most "successful" people profiled in the UK magazine *Stylist* get up at 6 a.m. and often work into the evening. Apple CEO Tim Cook told *Time* magazine that he begins his day at 3:45 a.m.[12] It seems odd that working insane hours is still something to brag about, that it's still seen in some way as equaling success. We have a long way to go, but, slowly, things are changing.

Human beings aren't meant to always be on. I love Laura Archer's book, *Gone for Lunch: 52 Things to Do in Your Lunch Break,* and the accompanying campaign to encourage people to actually take their lunch break. This break is an important time to fuel your mind and body for phase two of the working day. Similarly, I love this inspirational quote I've seen in my social-media feeds: "There is literally nothing in nature that blooms all year long, so do not expect yourself to do so." It reminds me that we need to rest and grow.

HERE ARE SOME THINGS I DO TO EARN MORE AND WORK LESS
- » Cut down on travel time: Do not waste time traveling to meetings throughout the day. Either plan all your meetings in one part of the day or have conversations via Skype or Google Hangouts. Fiercely protect your commute time.
- » Clear parameters on time and fee: Always be very clear on how long something will take you to complete. If you're unsure, never pick a ballpark figure out of the air for a whole project and instead break down your fee by hour or day or half day. This means you won't do extra work for free. Value your time.
- » Outsource your administrative tasks: A PA used to be something that only a high-powered CEO would have, but not anymore. Virtual assistants can help with tasks that can suck your time, for example: data entry, transcription, scheduling, copywriting, programming, design. Virtual PAs are great because they can do the work as needed (they don't necessarily need to be retained) and they usually work at home and, in fact, they may never need to meet their clients in person.

Know Your Own Limits

Our energy levels and susceptibility to burnout might be different from those of our friends' or colleagues'. This is why work shaming is so unproductive. Work shaming is when you make someone feel bad for their work choices (even branding someone a "workaholic" isn't exactly supportive). There's no one-size-fits-all solution for everyone. It's really down to each individual's limits. You could hit burnout by doing one thing too many (saying yes to too many projects, meetings, or nights out, for example), but a friend might be in a particularly productive period and feel energized by having a lot of things going on. We all have a different idea of what balance is, and it should be a personal journey in discovering it.

Similarly, we all have our own limits when it comes to technology and social media. There is a tendency to make sweeping generalizations as to how we should deal with the overwhelming nature of these things. Many people feel that young people are ill-equipped for online life—there have been calls to ban under-eighteens from using social media without prior mental health training courses on how to deal with the Internet.[13] According to the *Guardian*, which published results from a government-funded study, an estimated one in four teenage girls is reported as suffering from depression or anxiety, which is a rise of 10 percent on figures from just ten years ago. It is a real problem, and I would never argue against wider availability of mental health resources, but does a social-media ban address these serious issues? Surely, it would make more sense to give young people more access to advice, tips, and tools on how to deal with burnout or feeling overwhelmed.

We need to get better at teaching ourselves and those around us to filter information effectively so that we are not overwhelmed by endless information. Tom Friedman said it well: without effective filters, "the Internet, the mother of all flows, is actually an open sewer of untreated, unfiltered information."[14] We are wading through so much rubbish online daily—no wonder it is making us exhausted. But there are some simple ways in which we can better manage our time spent online and combat the feeling of being overwhelmed.

HERE ARE SOME TOOLS FOR CURATING YOUR ONLINE ENVIRONMENT

> » "Unfollow" or "mute" that annoying person or brand online that feels too intrusive. You aren't unfriending, and it's not a

cull; you are simply hiding it from your feed. You can also mute keywords on platforms like Twitter.

» Remove push notifications on apps you don't want daily (or hourly) updates from.

» Save articles you want to read into an app like Pocket (which you can also get as an extension on your browser) or instapaper.com so you can read everything at the end of the day or the next morning. This means you're not constantly consuming or getting notifications.

» Use simplenote.com to store notes across all your devices so you don't have to email yourself and risk getting distracted with something else.

» Something like nuzzel.com helps you curate your own news discovery. You save time by getting the best and most relevant information sent straight to you.

Is Social Media the New Smoking?

"It's not hard for me to imagine that in 20 years from now we find that what social media does to our brains is equivalent to what smoking does to our lungs."
—YANCEY STRICKLER, Kickstarter CEO[15]

I often find myself sitting in a towel on my bed after I've gotten out of the shower, scrolling mindlessly on my phone, almost in a daze, unable to stop. I'm not comfortable with this fact. I love technology, and my career is built around it, but I strive for balance and using tech as a tool to help me. In order not to burn out, it's important that we establish some ground rules when it comes to our tech. That doesn't mean undergoing extravagant digital-detox packages that are sold to us. We shouldn't have to spend hard-earned money on a weekend away without our phone. Back when I worked at a well-known women's magazine, we would get pitched "Ten ways to do a digital detox!" about twenty times a week. What irritated me about these ideas on how to switch off was they were always predicated on something expensive: a yoga retreat, an expensive leather bag that turns off your notifications, a faraway health resort run by a wellness guru. It always seemed like a rip-off, and I wasn't convinced that any of these things were actually going to help people in their day-to-day lives. Call me old-fashioned but I don't think mindfulness should have to come with a massive price tag.

It's the mindless scrolling that is the hard thing to kick to the curb. Leading a multi-hyphenate lifestyle involves a lot of self-motivation, so addressing your social-media scrolling addiction is crucial. To work less and earn more means being really strict with your social-media usage. It means scheduling content more than posting it manually, to avoid spending too much time on the platforms.

It certainly feels like we are living in a time where everything is "urgent." Writer Lynn Enright summed this up in a piece for the Pool: "There is a lot of urgency around: there is a greedy internet to fill with content; there are other media outlets to best and beat; there are ideas, tidbits, pictures and rumors, on Twitter and in inboxes and WhatsApp groups, and they might be urgent, you've got to check."[16] It feels so good to rebel against someone else's urgency, someone else's ASAP alerts. In order to make something that lives on, that might mean something or even make us money in the long run, we can't fall into the trap of wasting all of our time on Snapchat or Instagram Stories. Sometimes it can feel like we are hamsters trapped in a wheel, clicking on the content that we have to watch immediately otherwise it might disappear.

True productivity occurs when we are aware of what our bodies are doing. We waste time when we go and get that millionth coffee from the kitchen at work; we also waste time when we mindlessly scroll through social media. Having a healthy relationship with our devices is about being aware of our time wasting as it happens. Do you start scrolling and then realize a large chunk of time has vanished? Do you try for an early night and find yourself reading the entire World Wide Web before bed? Do your eyes ache from too much screen time? Do your eyes glaze over? Do you find yourself looking at stuff that makes you feel bad about yourself? I think the way to address these behaviors is more about taking control of our daily lives than going cold turkey or "curing" ourselves of our addictions. It's about being mindful of the signs that we are online too much; it's catching ourselves while we're in the trap. It's being more aware; it's stopping ourselves as we reach for our phones yet again and asking ourselves why we're doing it.

The term "addiction" is no exaggeration. We get hits of dopamine every time we get a like, comment, or notification—many studies have said that we feel the same when we get a positive online notification as we do a hug. The average person checks his or her smartphone 150 times a day, making more than 2,000 swipes and touches.[17] The heaviest smartphone users click, tap, or swipe on their phone 5,427 times a day, according to researcher Dscout.[18]

Surely, being so addicted is not making us very productive in office spaces, where we are expected to sit and work all day with constant distractions. We need to get better at disconnecting. However, if our attention spans are being diminished and we also have multiple metaphorical tabs open at all times, then the rise of the Multi-Hyphen Life makes sense. It allows you to concentrate on one thing at a time, but you get to decide how many of those things you have going at any given time and how long you want to spend on each one. When working for yourself, you're more aware of time and output, often because you are working on things yourself without a huge team. You're much less likely to want to spend precious hours wasting time on your phone because you're working on your own passion projects, where before you might have scrolled through dead hours when there was less to do in the office.

There are interesting recent studies about young people and tech. Shocking admissions are coming from whistleblowers at tech giants who are confessing that they know how addictive their online products can be. The *Guardian* profiled Justin Rosenstein, an American software programmer who created the "like" button when he was an engineer at Facebook. The interview revealed a lot about the ways tech platforms work to keep us hooked, like spacing out push notifications and gamifying the experience of social networking (hearts, likes, polls, shares) to keep us checking our phones more frequently. The article revealed that "younger technologists are weaning themselves off their own products, sending their children to elite Silicon Valley schools where iPhones, iPads, and even laptops are banned."[19] Another former Facebook employee, Chamath Palihapitiya, who left in 2011, admitted that "we have created tools that are ripping apart the social fabric of how society works."[20] The most disturbing revelation was that mindless scrolling isn't something we've accidentally fallen into; it is apparently all "just as their designers [at the tech giants] intended." Though upsetting to read, the upside of all this honesty might be that younger generations will be more aware of the not-so-altruistic motivations behind the tech we use and the consequences of the way we use it. Self-awareness and self-analysis are the first steps to not letting tech control as much of your life. And being more aware of how the tech actually operates—and the ways it's intended to manipulate our attention—is the next step to avoiding being sucked into it for life. If you know more about a platform or device's design, we can take action to combat its influence. British businesswoman and philanthropist Martha Lane Fox champions this as well, urging us to "educate our children by teaching them as much as we can about technology. We need to go beyond basic skills to raise the first generation of native digital understanders— people who, unlike most of the rest of us, know where and how their technology is made."[21] In order to be truly empowered and emboldened by technology, we have to understand it more deeply, or we risk mindlessly becoming addicted while not looking beneath the surface of what it's doing to us and why.

Beyond sucking up our time and attention, endless scrolling, through the news in particular, is also making a lot of us sick. There are many studies showing the correlation between the twenty-four-hour news cycle and increased anxiety. The pace of information is relentless. Journalist Jess Commons recently wrote for *Refinery29*:

"A few months ago, I, a fully grown-up, functional human woman, had to take nearly a month off work in the wake of the rising tensions between Kim Jong-un and Donald Trump. I know it sounds ridiculous to say out loud, but from the 'fire and fury' day, I was a mess. I spent days sitting on my couch, crying, not eating and watching rubbish movies. No matter what anyone said to me, I could not get my anxiety under control."[22]

Our phones can make brilliant things happen, but they can also be the source of a lot of anxiety. It's time to take control. We need to set our own personal limits and not feel bad for switching off.

I definitely feel my best self when I've had time off; I feel refreshed and motivated, and I'm full of ideas and am ready to solve new problems. It's simply not possible to give 100 percent all the time.

THE POWER OF TAKING BREAKS

» Taking breaks boosts our creativity.

» Stepping away from a project and turning your attention to another one that requires a different skill or way of using your brain make you better at your job.

» Brief diversions from a task can dramatically improve someone's ability to focus on that task for extended periods of time.[23]

» Mindfulness expert Andy Puddicombe advocates the transformative power of taking ten minutes to do absolutely nothing. Harder than it sounds but so worth it.

EMBRACE SLOW LIVING

"Slow living" sounds like a buzzword, but it's so much more than that. Slow living is essentially about taking a slower approach to aspects of everyday life. It's about embracing a lifestyle that is the opposite of the "now-if-not-sooner" culture we're accustomed to: slow communication, slow food, slow fashion, slow life. It's a lifestyle that is quite difficult to practice because of the nature of the world we now live in, where a news story breaks on social media before it is verified and information spreads like wildfire.

I asked the renowned photographer and popular Instagrammer Sara Tasker for her thoughts on slow living. She has amassed a huge following of hundreds of thousands for displaying her life through a slow-life lens. Her Instagram account @me_and_orla is about slowing down and celebrating quiet moments. She said:

"I see slow living as the antidote to the glorification of 'busyness.' It's doing things the hard way sometimes—walking not driving, sweeping not hoovering, or just watching the rain on the window instead of checking our phones—as a way to be mindful and stop rushing ahead. The Internet is great for connecting with others around us, but we still need these moments of quietness to connect to ourselves and to the great history of humans who also walked, swept, and watched the rain sometimes. In a world that equates productivity with worthiness, doing things the slow way can be a rebellious act."

TIPS FOR INCORPORATING ASPECTS OF SLOW LIVING INTO YOUR LIFE

» If you find yourself refreshing/scrolling/in zombie mode, pause. Close your eyes and stop for a moment. Become aware of these moments and stop yourself from being vacantly transfixed.
» Take just a small moment for yourself each morning. Lie in bed for a few minutes doing nothing before grabbing your phone to scroll through Instagram.
» Embrace boredom. Allow yourself to be bored sometimes— you'll be surprised what your brain gets up to.
» Leave the house early and walk to your meeting or meetup with friends.

» Watch a film at home, go for dinner, and put your phone in a drawer.

» Identify and write down when you see something online that makes you feel less than or overly jealous or miserable. These are what comparison coach Lucy Sheridan calls your "comparison triggers."

» Be properly present at mealtimes (and when you're cooking and eating).

» Listen to podcasts instead of checking your emails on the commute.

The first challenge is working out our own personal boundaries and deciding what's feasible, the second is our employers setting boundaries by example, and third is owning our choices and maintaining the balance.

It's time we slowed down and looked up from our devices a bit more. Small steps are better than nothing.

Chapter 6

THE WORK-LIFE BLEND

Is blending your work life and home life together good or bad? Not an easy or straightforward question to answer. On the one hand, blending the two means you can lead more of a balanced life because strict separation is difficult to do for everyone nowadays. Maybe you blend your work and home life already, for example, by working from home some days, keeping unconventional office hours, doing your laundry in between emails, picking up a family member in the afternoon, or splitting up your day however you please and having more flexibility on a micro level. This sounds great in many ways, having that flexibility to shape work around your life and not the other way around. We have the technology that allows us to be more flexible and to have a working life that can suit our individual needs and personal lives. But, on the other hand, it can be dangerous because you can overwork yourself without clear boundaries between work and rest. I'm a fan of the blended approach when done in a way that works for you. I think it is increasingly inevitable that we will blend work and home life more. According to a report this year from FlexJobs and Global Workplace Analytics, there's been a 115 percent increase in the United States in people who work, at least in some part, from home since 2005—jumping from 1.8 million to 3.9 million.[1]

We have the tools to make a blended life work. However, we don't want to draw the short straw and end up blending our lives for not much professional gain. I'm interested in how we tackle it, manage it, stay sane, and be in control of how much we blend our lives and why.

Blurred Lines

Right now, we are merging way more than we think. There are countless people who argue that blending work and home life is very bad and the two should remain entirely separate, but they write emails on the way into work on the train. The very nature of having a portable phone means you are already blurring the lines. Perhaps you are checking Twitter on the weekend with the aim of building the platform of your business. Is this play (because you might be live-tweeting some funny one-liners from *Bake Off*) or work (because you are attracting new followers)? Even if you don't have a flexible setup, if you reply to emails in your off hours or you quickly check something work related while sitting on the sofa watching reality shows, you are technically blurring your work and home life, probably without realizing. With all the tech we have in our lives, it's not so simple to make work and home life completely separate. And it's a pretty recent problem—the idea of opting to have work emails on your phone is a newish thing—so we don't yet have the answers.

Twitter European Vice President Bruce Daisley said in a *Times* interview that "since the advent of email on mobile phones enabled us to check our inboxes continually, the working day has increased from seven and a half hours to nine and a half."[2] This suggests that most people's current blend is having us work more without any extra pay (unless you are self-employed or have a strict hourly fee). We just sit back and accept that work will bleed into our home life. It doesn't seem fair.

Work and Life

Work can seep into our personal spaces without our inviting it in. For example, if our partner or best friend is having a horrible time at work, it can impact the way we think about our own job, and we can affect their relationship with their work too. A German study by Hahn and Dormann of 114 couples who both worked found that "one person's after-hours psychological detachment from work was associated with their partner's own detachment from their work. There was a big correlation between the couple's feelings and emotions to do with work, suggesting that we are impressionable and we take on other people's feelings. If your other half finds it easy to switch off when they get home, then you will probably find it easier too, which is beneficial for your family and work life."[3]

This, to me, is another example showing that true separation between our work and our home life is a myth. They have always interwoven and intertwined in some way, and they have always been connected; to think you can slice it down the middle is naive. If you need to rant about work woes or your boss, I find it helps to leave the house to talk about it with a friend or partner. Go for a walk, go out for food, or take a stroll to the shops. This helps you get it out of your system and means you aren't letting negative work energy into your living room. The blend of work energy is something to keep a close eye on.

We may never be able to totally switch off from work, but we can find tools to help us make work less stressful and overwhelming. Having multiple hyphens to your career means you never need to feel totally invested in just one thing because your time is spread between multiple projects. Projects have shorter windows because you have many different jobs, and, therefore, you know that soon you'll be on to the next thing with a fresh start and new sense of energy. A lot of my work dread came from feeling trapped by feeling permanently attached to one job.

When I worked in social media, tweeting for big brands and national magazines, I never, ever switched off. I wasn't a nurse on call, but I treated my corporate marketing job like it was the most important thing in the world. Being young in a new job and trying to prove yourself are scary. You feel like you should always be "on." Understanding healthy boundaries is not something you innately know. Part of my role was to keep myself updated across all of the brands' social-media channels, monitoring positive comments, negative comments, and crisis-management scenarios (aka someone saying something highly damaging about the company). I would have to flag the damaging comments to the CEO, and we'd decide as a team how best to deal with them. I felt on edge all the time. No one teaches you how to deal with this "always-on" mentality when you are in school. I grew up thinking that work and time off were totally separate, with work being something you could close the door on when you left your desk for the day. But for so many of us, work can seep into all areas of our lives, and we can feel overwhelmed very quickly.

My work-life blend was really unhealthy. I couldn't tell the difference between work and home life because the phone in my pocket was always buzzing. I'd be out of town at my nephew's birthday party, bouncing up and down on a seesaw or jumping in a ball pit, and my phone would go off. "There's an issue that needs handling right this moment" the email subject line would read, and I would feel a metaphorical punch in the stomach as I missed out on special moments with my family to deal with the problem. I had to ask myself then, *Is this really what I want my career to look like? Isn't it only going to get worse?*

The thing is, you don't have to work in social media or have a job like the one I just described to have that gut-punch feeling when you're off work and something urgent comes up. Most of us have been emailed in our off hours by a frantic boss who expects a reply. To be contactable at all times makes us anxious. I've been in many work environments where the busier you are, the later you work, and the more visible you are in the team's inboxes mean you are considered the better employee. But this isn't true. Learning what is genuinely urgent and what is masquerading as being urgent is a skill in itself.

We are working more than we think. If you have a public Instagram or Twitter account, you are (perhaps without realizing) promoting yourself and your brand to the world, and you are somewhat "on." Because my work-life balance was so bad when I worked at corporations, I realized that if there was going to be such a blurred boundary, I would build it on my own terms. I would treat this off-hours work as investing in myself, and, whatever the outcome, I—not the company—would reap the rewards. It wasn't necessarily flipping the bird to "the man," but if I was going to be "always on" in this tech-obsessed, status-obsessed, ratings-obsessed world, I was going to do it my way. I would treat every click, hour, late night, and blurred line as an investment in myself and the projects I would one day run. It was my way of justifying the work overload. At least I would have something to always fall back on: my own personal brands and skills.

I want to talk about the pros and cons and how to handle this work-life blend because I think it is crucial to the future of work conversation. I think we are going to be blending our lives more, not less, in the future. Instead of dreaming of the old days, I believe we have to move forward and learn how to deal with the blend. When I was a teenager with a Nokia 3210, no one could really disturb me except for a simple text every now and again. It was normal not to have a signal or for my phone to be off. Now I have an iPhone, and there is often no reason I can't reply immediately. If someone doesn't get a reply within thirty minutes, it's not uncommon to receive a follow-up with "Did you get this? Just a gentle reminder." There's nothing gentle about nudging an email less than an hour after it's been sent. And don't get me started on read notifications. The expectations of responsiveness have risen. People talk about the separation of work and home life, but that was back when you literally couldn't get ahold of your colleagues unless you sent a telegram or Hedwig or something. Technology has changed everything, and it's here to stay.

Commentator Will Self said something recently that made me shout "OOOOF" at my laptop. We think work and leisure are separate entities, but they are not: "The idea of not-working and working are locked into an unholy and reciprocal relationship with each other. The fact that you're not working is only because you've been working, and the fact that you're working is only so you can not work."[4] We work so we can have time off. Time off exists only when we have work. Aristotle said: "We work to have leisure, on which happiness depends." I believe the Multi-Hyphen Life is the best way to merge the two and have some leisure time while we work, to be more in control of your work-life blend. Why does it have to be two total extremes? Conventional wisdom is that we will be happy only when we retire or reach that career nirvana we've all been striving for—but, surely, we should try to have some fun along the way too.

Workin' Nine-to-Five

In 1969, Charles Bukowski famously wrote a letter to his publisher John Martin and spoke of his elation at being able to escape his full-time job:

"It's never 9 to 5, there's no free lunch break at those places, in fact, at many of them in order to keep your job you don't take lunch. Then there's OVERTIME and the books never seem to get the overtime right and if you complain about that, there's another sucker to take your place."

A nine-to-five has never been a nine-to-five, and technology has made "overtime" even worse. With the Multi-Hyphen Life, instead of five days of solid work and two days of solid fun, each day can level out a bit, and work and fun can merge more successfully. I've been able to make up my own workweek rules and my own weekend rules. This is not to say that every day or week is perfectly balanced. But I wanted to even out the two extremes. Some weeks I might work six days; some weeks I might work three. Some weeks I might sleep in most days; some weeks I might be up at 6 a.m. to travel. It's a totally different way of looking at the working week—it is up to you how much you want to work or not work. It's up to you to plan ahead and avoid underworking and overworking, depending on the projects you take on. I used to be miserable all through the week, with only a slight bit of sunshine and happiness on the weekend. I used to feel euphoric on Friday evenings and then get the Sunday scaries at lunchtime on a Sunday. I didn't want to live for the weekend anymore. This is not to say I don't still have bad days. Life is life. Work is work. But I am more likely to have a good day off and a good day at work now. Perhaps the question isn't "Is the work-life blend bad?" but "How much are we blending, and where's the line?" We need to make sure we are blending in a productive way and not just because we can.

THREE WAYS TO AVOID BLENDING TOO MUCH

1. Even if you're not in an office, set office hours: Having a multi-hyphenate job enables flexibility, but you still need office hours or some sort of structure. Make sure you set yourself a time frame for working, and if it spills over slightly, that's OK, but you need to have some sense of when to put your laptop away; otherwise, you'll carry on working and it'll feel never-ending.

2. Have a social-media-free lunch break: This applies to any work setup. Have a complete break in the middle of the day— it helps to have a period of no work and no social media.

3. Hold yourself accountable to someone else: If you know that you might skip the lunch, the fresh air, the walk, the break in the day, the evening off, etc., then make plans to see a friend or family member so that you are accountable to someone else.

Trust Is Key

One question that arises in terms of the Multi-Hyphen Life is how to communicate to your primary boss that you might have an outside-of-work side hustle. This happened in a few of my roles. A boss once asked me about my own projects, and I could see she was worried that it might be distracting me from my day job. She knew that I was doing other projects, like writing for magazines in the evenings, because she was friends with me on Facebook. She wanted to bring it up, because she didn't understand how I was finding the time to do it, and I thought it was strange that she wanted to know, considering I was getting all of my work done. But, eventually, it did get to the point where I had to make a choice because the side projects took on a life of their own. This time I initiated the conversation and communicated with my boss about transitioning out of my role. I would have been happy working on my hobby and having my full-time job because I enjoyed it, but my projects outpaced my job. That's the exciting thing about side projects: They can be small and nourishing, but they can also turn into something bigger.

Sometimes, your boss might have an issue with your outside-of-work projects, but I think as the workplace continues to evolve, bosses will have to be more open with their employees who have portfolio careers or other income streams. The web-hosting company GoDaddy surveyed a thousand millennials and a thousand baby boomers in the United States about side hustles. They found that one in two millennials and one in four baby boomers have one.[5] In the past year, Google Trends shows that searches for "side hustle" have increased 138 percent in the United Kingdom and 178 percent in the United States.[6] It is so much easier to beta test an idea or set up a business online that it is to be expected that people are going to explore their options.

Our employers are entitled to know where we are within our contracted work hours, but I can't help but wonder whether this needs to change and that trust between employer and employees needs to strengthen. This is especially the case if more employees are going to be working flexibly—a level of trust is needed. As long as the work is getting done and is being done well, I think employers should trust their employees to manage their own time. I remember once having to tell my male boss in detail about my gynecologist appointments because he needed to know exactly why I needed time off during the week. There is nothing more important than our health—that's not up for debate. Without our health, we are useless to our employers. Why can't we let each other leave the office for personal reasons, believing and knowing that as diligent employees we are still getting the job done?

In this new public social-media age, we know more about our colleagues than we did pre-Internet. We are more visible, and I think we should be more open. A promising example of this is a tweet that went viral in 2016 by Madalyn Parker, a web developer from a Michigan-based software company who left an out-of-office message for colleagues explaining she needed a break from work to "focus on her mental health," which was received brilliantly by her boss, Ben Congleton. He praised her as an "example to us all" in an email that went out to the company about the importance of talking about mental health.[7] Life doesn't stop just because we have a work deadline. For example, Nike introduced menstrual leave in 2007, so why are these normal human things still controversial? I think it highlights the fact that workplaces still find it difficult to give employees flexibility on any level.

The Importance of Setting Clear Boundaries

Boundaries are incredibly important, especially if you work from home. According to BizReport, one recent survey on remote workers showed that 38 percent wake up at some point during the night to check their email.[8] This is not good for anyone. If you reply in the middle of the night, your boss or colleague is learning that it's fine to expect instant replies at crazy times. Just because we can do more with technology and we can be online all the time doesn't mean we should be. Just because someone emails us doesn't mean we have to reply straightaway. The expected amount of time that is "normal" to wait for a reply is becoming shorter and shorter. Without boundaries, we are at the beck and call of our devices—an endless loop of Internetting.

It should be up to us to choose whether we want to blend our work into the evenings or days off. A good boundary is one you create for yourself. It's one thing if you want to dip into some work one evening, another if you feel like you might get fired if you don't. Again, it is the psychology and emotions behind the blend. Leaders and bosses should lead the way and show that it's possible to have a healthy balance.

If your boss is not leading by example, it's very hard to implement your own rules. The Internet has stripped us of our natural physical boundaries. We can be accessed at all times, we are always connected in some way, and we know whether someone has read something, so we need our employers (even if you are your own boss) to enforce some boundaries to follow. When I had bosses who also had outside-of-work projects or hobbies, it really improved my mental health in the office because they understood that there's more to life than just your time in the office.

To some, the idea of flexibility or remote working means that you could be opening up the possibility for your boss (or colleagues, contacts, etc.) to constantly ask you for stuff in a way that feels more stressful or overbearing. Because you are available online as a desktop icon and not in person, it may feel more intrusive to be instant messaged rather than having a quick face-to-face chat in the office. This is why no matter your work setup, you need to determine some hard and soft boundaries. For me, online boundaries are just as important as physical ones.

THREE TIPS FOR SETTING BOUNDARIES

1. Manage expectations: Let your team/colleagues know that you won't be on WhatsApp or any other messenger during certain times but you will reply as soon as you can.

2. Put an out-of-office on: A friendly out-of-office is a great way to ease off emails for an afternoon. You don't have to be on holiday for an out-of-office. I put one on if I'm having a hectic day, and it makes me feel less stressed.

3. Have premade answers you can link to: In your out-of-office you can preemptively answer questions. For example: "If you are writing about X, please be in touch with this person," "If you're asking about Y initiative, I wrote a blog post about it here." It's almost like a FAQ.

HOW MUCH DO YOU LIKE TO BLEND WORK AND PLAY?

Just as work is different for some people, so is downtime. What relaxes you might not relax someone else. For example, my nephew hates sitting still. If I asked him to sit still in a chair for an afternoon, he would not be relaxed in the slightest. Give him a ball to kick around a park and he'd be relaxed in an instant. We are all different. We shouldn't feel like we need to be productive with our downtime. We don't always need to track our meditation like it's a work project or clock our sleep on an app or feel pressured to finish a book. Society tells us to achieve in every area of our lives, be it work or play. But downtime is personal. Figure out what it looks like for you.

ANSWER THESE QUESTIONS TO WORK OUT WHAT YOUR BOUNDARIES ARE

» In what situations do you not mind someone emailing you about something work related?

» Are you always sure what is work and what is play, or can they merge easily?

» What is your hard "rest" boundary—that is, it is never OK to do work during this particular time?

» What is your soft "rest" boundary—that is, you wouldn't mind doing some work during this particular time? What kind of work would that be, and why?

» Do fun WhatsApp groups with colleagues count as working to you?

» Do work parties count as work time to you?

» What noises help you work? Music, white noise, silence?

» Do you prefer working in big or small groups?

Try to find the common themes from your answers that you can turn into a set of "rules" that can also help you find the time for your other side projects or hyphens. For example:

» I will not answer emails after 7 p.m.
» I will not check my emails on the way to work.
» I will put my phone on airplane mode during time spent on my side project.

Work Perks? Spot the Traps

In some cases, employers use flexibility to try to suck up more of your time. They may try to pretend they offer flexibility, but, really, they're expecting us to work overtime and all the time. For example, the idea of unlimited vacation time, on paper, seems amazing, but it often means you are expected to pay for the perk by being endlessly contactable or you have to make up the time elsewhere. In 2014 the BBC reported that Richard Branson was going to give all of his employees unlimited vacation at the Virgin Group. It seems like this would totally align choosing productivity over presenteeism. Branson said: "We should focus on what people get done, not on how many hours or days worked. Just as we don't have a nine-to-five policy, we don't need a vacation policy."[9] I liked the sound of it, a lot. Of course, it's often too good to be true. Aaron McEwan, HR advisory leader at CEB, said that employees don't end up taking much vacation because the actual workload doesn't practically allow for a lot of time off or they're worried about their colleagues' perceptions: "The likelihood of people taking more leave just because there's a policy is actually really low." Ted Livingston, CEO of Kik Messenger said: "We found 'take as much as you want' actually did the reverse—people took less. The dirty little secret is that nobody will take vacation—it's the nobody-takes-vacation policy. We said, 'We're going to have a must-take-vacation policy.'"[10]

Some perks—like sleep pods, game rooms, etc.—are designed to keep workers in the office longer. I've never felt comfortable with this. The major players in Silicon Valley were described in the *Guardian* as "fun palaces instead of offices and offer on-demand massages and you get a company razor scooter in the welcome pack."[11] It can get more invasive. Facebook, for example, offers to freeze your eggs for you. Is this empowering, or is it a way to encourage you to put your personal life on hold in service of the company?

Of course, it's a feminist issue too. Journalist Suzanne Moore explained:

"The structure of the workplace is still not meeting the needs of women, and the culture is not producing men who meet the desires of generations of women who thought they could have it all. So we end up with huge corporations offering female employees the possibility of reproduction at a later date in return for the 'best' years of their lives. This hardly strikes me as a perk. It is a bribe."[12]

These perks—endless vacation, beers in the office fridge, on-site bar, game consoles—are all means to justify a fifty-plus-hour week, instead of letting their employees have a life outside of work. In my past jobs there were free ski trips, office parties, table tennis. These are all fine if they happen within the confines of normal work hours, but to offer them so that employees never leave feels quite dark.

In Miya Tokumitsu's book *Do What You Love*, she says that making employees feel like they love their job has also become a method of exploitation. Hiding behind this mantra, employers are able to squeeze even more work out of their employees. This is another example of why it is dangerous to put all your eggs in one career basket.

Taking Your Work Home vs. Taking Your Work Stress Home

I recently read something that made me realize that taking "work" home and taking "work stress" home are two very different things. An article on Girlboss stated: "Taking your work home with you in the evening is one thing, but bringing the toxicity of work stress with you can mess up your family life and relationships in a major way." This is a mental challenge more than anything. There is a difference between bringing work tasks home—such as a project that you could perhaps do in your living room—and bringing the stressful environment or feelings of the workplace. Letting any sort of bad vibes into your home from work can be upsetting. I remember being deeply upset on one vacation because of an email I'd received from a colleague. We were connected on Facebook, and every time I logged on, I was visually reminded of her existence and the email she'd sent; it really ruined my holiday. We are not able to switch off from our workplace feelings so easily. I'm sure "out of sight, out of mind" worked much better before the Internet.

A lot of people fear that working from home or working in the evenings could lead to burnout and overwhelm, which is understandable. But, on the other hand, when working on outside-of-work projects or working on work tasks on your own schedule, there can be positives in working from home or in the evenings (if you are a night owl).

Get a Work-Life Fit, Not Balance

I was on a panel with Sarah Jackson, the CEO of the UK nonprofit Working Families, and she said that "work-life balance" often makes us feel guilty because balance is hard to measure and it's different for everyone. Balance for one person might mean having more time for their children, balance for someone else might mean having more vacations, and for someone else it might mean more time for their side projects or hobbies. Instead, Sarah talked about "work-life fit," which I think feels like a healthier work-life model.

An entrepreneur on the panel was asked, "Do you try to get some balance in your life to prepare you for when you might have kids?" The entrepreneur replied, "How do you know whether I want to have kids?"

We often assume that we all want a variation on the same thing, but what works for us might not work for other people. Your own work-life fit is unique to you.

The reason the work-life fit approach suits the Multi-Hyphen Life is because you are able to design your own schedule, the start and end points of your workweek, and where you work. Blended approaches can be positive when you are self-employed or working on a side hustle because you reap the benefits of any extra time you put in. But too much blend when you are working for one employer can end up being exploitative and can lead to burnout because, ultimately, you are not in control and your extra effort is only for your company's gain. You are letting work blend into your life for someone else's benefit.

TIPS ON ADJUSTING YOUR BLEND

» If you've blended your workweek and weekends, make sure you give yourself time off; that is, if you worked on a project on a Sunday night from home, give yourself a break one weekday afternoon—and don't feel guilty about it!

» Always take a day off if you worked a day on your own time— even if you work for yourself.

» Track your hours, have a weekly limit in mind, and stick to it. Just because you're blending doesn't mean you should work more hours.

» Make sure you are taking on projects that won't suck your time too much. Have a solid contract in place up front that clearly outlines how much time you will spend on it.

Chapter 7

MULTI-HYPHEN LIFE TOOL KIT

Ten Ways to Lay Your Multi-Hyphenate Foundations

1. PINPOINT YOUR OWN UNIQUE BLEND

The first thing to do is figure out what your new "job title" is. It might be helpful to draw inspiration from some of the multi-hyphenates featured in this book, but, ultimately, your mix will look different from others'. Follow the steps below to help you define what your mixture is and how to build confidence around selling yourself as a multi-hyphenate:

» Write a list of words you'd like to be described as.
» Write a list of things you'd like to be recognized for or any side projects you'd like to start or continue. You might find that you have a list of around five different things that could be job titles or separate skills, and that's OK.
» Write a list of all the things you are good at. These can be small things, like that you are tidy, or a good host, or good at listening. These are all important, because the things you are good at (however random or varied) can play a role in your multi-hyphenate career. A lot of our skills don't get used when we have just one job.
» Find the common themes in your different skills. You may be surprised that your random assortment of skills will actually

make sense when you add them up. They will complement each other in a way you wouldn't have previously thought of. Take the part-time podcast host and part-time chef featured in chapter 3—creating a great new recipe out of many different ingredients is a skill similar to chopping up bits of audio and making a compelling new narrative. The links between your two jobs might not be obvious, but when you dig more deeply, they will be revealed.

» Practice referring to yourself out loud with your new mix of job titles. You are a well-rounded person with many different skills. Be confident with it. Cass Business School professor Stefan Stern says, "What people do is more important than what they are called. So we should probably all lighten up a bit about job titles. The crucial thing is to be able to understand what someone does without referring to a dictionary."[1]

» Practice defining your multi-hyphenate career in different ways. Depending on your environment, different strands of your job will be more relevant than others, especially if they're in very different industries. The beauty of a multi-hyphenate career is that you can wear different hats, depending on the situation, circumstance, or commission.

Tip: If you have a hard time finding your writing voice (whether you are trying to write website copy, a proposal, notes for this part of the tool kit, anything), record yourself speaking in voice notes on your phone or into a Dictaphone (I recommended a Zoom mic) and transcribe them afterward. It will help you focus, relax, and find your true voice. I find speaking out loud helps me really believe in and manifest what I'm saying.

2. GROW AND MAINTAIN A MICRO-AUDIENCE

Being a multi-hyphenate is not about being an "influencer"; it is about developing an authentic and real audience of people who know you for doing what you do. They could be connections on LinkedIn who might hire you in the future, or Twitter followers who might invite you to do some work for them, or like-minded people you can add to your professional network. Or maybe they're new friends you cultivate without a professional agenda. Social media is amazing, and each and every one of us gets to grow communities if we want.

However, there are traps you can fall into when you have any sort of "following." Try to avoid becoming complacent and putting too much weight on one platform. What happens if your Instagram account gets deleted overnight? Or if it becomes less popular in the future? Vine was once a huge platform, with the biggest Vine stars attracting partnerships with major companies and brands, and then one day Vine just didn't exist anymore. Imagine spending years making your Myspace page amazing, and cultivating an audience there, only for Myspace users to suddenly leave en masse for Facebook. That happened.

Being a successful multi-hyphenate relies on getting different kinds of work by being known to people who can give you that work. It doesn't mean having thousands of followers or being famous. It means being known within your field(s) and industry landscape. It's not about being a #girlboss with millions of loyal acolytes; it's about hanging your proverbial shingle above your door and saying, "Come in; let's work together!"

Growing a micro-audience is really important for your business, but here is the crunch: It has to be real, which is why it's good to aim small. Having a smaller, more engaged audience for your work, made up of mostly people who are interested in working with you (aka potential future employers), is ideal. Big numbers don't really matter here. Because who cares if you have one million followers if only a tiny proportion of them care about what you're doing or saying? Newsletters have grown in popularity for this very reason. Having a thousand people genuinely interested in hearing from you in their inbox is much more powerful than having hundreds of thousands of passive Instagram followers.

TIPS ON GROWING A MICRO-AUDIENCE

» Listen and respond. Don't treat social media like a bullhorn to only broadcast about yourself.

» Ask yourself, WHY am I posting this? Always have a reason. If you don't, then message that picture, post, question to a friend instead.

» "Authenticity" is an overused word these days, but be human. People can spot if you're trying too hard to be "real" too, so just try to be as close to your IRL self as possible.

» Arrange small events or meetups (in collaboration with like-minded people if you don't want to do it alone). Ask people to bring a friend to widen the net.

» Offer proper value—whether that's opportunities, information, giveaways—and always think back to the WHY.

» Start a newsletter. It's always been the best way to have an engaged small community away from the noise of public social-media platforms.

» Quality over quantity in terms of both numbers of followers and how often you post. Don't feel like you need to post every day just for the sake of it.

Confidence-boost tip: You don't need a huge online network to make a huge impact. In Tim Ferriss's book, *Tribe of Mentors*, writer Tim Urban said, "If only one in every thousand of [Internet users]—0.1 percent—happens to be a reader, that amounts to over a million people who will absolutely love what you're doing."[2] This quote stuck with me—I find it uplifting because it points to the fact that you don't need a huge percentage of any group of people (Internet users, book readers, etc.) to be into your thing, as even the tiniest fraction can be a lot of people.

3. ALWAYS BE IN BETA MODE

We can no longer plan ahead the way we used to because of the pace of new advancements in technology and the workplace. We must remain agile, whether we're working on our own, on a small team, or in a huge business. There is no way you can learn everything in one internal training course and then be an expert forever. This section is inspired by Reid Hoffman, founder of LinkedIn, whose mantra "Always be in beta" means act like you are never really finished improving. We are all always learning when it comes to tech and the new world of work, and none of us is going to be able to skip the hard work of continuously improving and rebranding ourselves over the years. In an interview with Deloitte on the future of work, *New York Times* columnist Tom Friedman said, "Never think of yourself as 'finished'; otherwise you really will be finished."[3]

We'll never totally master anything because there's always more to learn, and that's OK. By being in "beta mode," you are more likely to pivot or try something new. If you take this approach to your work, it will mean that you are also more likely to be an early adopter (a person who starts using a product or technology as soon as it becomes available), which can be crucial in getting ahead. If we stagnate and feel like we already know everything there is to know, we are at risk of falling behind. "How to stay in beta mode" ends up being "how to stay relevant."

HOW TO STAY IN BETA MODE

» Online courses, webinars, and lessons are crucial for beefing up your résumé and learning new skills like video, Photoshop, coding, languages, or photography. For example:

Khan Academy offers free online courses on just about every subject, including math, computing, art history, grammar, economics, personal finance, and even entrepreneurship.

Skillshare is a learning platform that helps you learn new skills that will help you creatively, from photography to coding to Photoshop.

Elevate app is like doing workout circuit training for your brain, featuring over forty games that boost productivity and confidence and improve your skills in reading, concentration, memory, speaking, and listening.

» Use your audience as a focus group to test out new ideas. Something as easy as doing an Instagram Story poll (asking your audience to vote) can help inform a small (or big) decision relating to your project or business.

Being in beta mode and staying on your toes don't mean feeling like you constantly need to dramatically update or overhaul things all the time. All it takes are small tweaks along the way to stay fresh. For example, beta mode doesn't mean totally redesigning your website every few months, but it does mean having a look at what you could fine-tune or what new features/widgets have just been launched that you could easily add. Sign up to design newsletters and keep an eye on your favorite websites and see how they are evolving.

4. EMBRACE THE AGE OF PERSONALIZATION

We are in an era of personalization. Online recommendations are targeted at us (most of the time, they work well—until they get creepy). Our favorite websites remember our passwords, credit card information, and what we like buying. We curate Pinterest boards. We organize our online lives with as much rigor as our offline lives. If personalization (whether we like it or not) happens so seamlessly online, then why shouldn't we personalize our working lives to the same extent? This is what the Multi-Hyphen Life is about: personalizing our work lives—because we should be allowed to. There is no reason why our jobs can't be like a well-cut bespoke suit made especially to accentuate our best features.

IN WHAT WAYS CAN YOU BEGIN TO PERSONALIZE YOUR LIFE?

» Experiment with your working environment. Take the Myers-Briggs personality test, which helps indicate how you perceive the world around you and make decisions. Figure out how certain tweaks to your environment or team setup might affect your working life. For example, if you are more of an introvert, it makes sense that you really need breaks from a busy open-plan office or coworking space and need to find your own quiet den.

» Are there any traits of your current work style that make you feel guilty even though they work well for you? Are there ways of embracing these traits instead of mentally beating yourself up? For example, I work well in the later part of the evening. I've always felt guilty about this, but I decided to embrace it as part of my routine and not stress about not being a morning person. Another example is a friend of mine who likes her paper planner for work meetings and doesn't want to convert to an online calendar even though she's been made to feel like she must go digital. Make a list of all the things that work well for you as a personal routine and try embracing them as they are.

5. BE YOUR OWN PR AND MARKETING DEPARTMENT

What does your front of house look like? Everyone has a shop window, and everyone is judged by it. Our shop front used to be a résumé, a piece of paper written in boring Times New Roman. Your first impression used to be the interview itself: a good shirt, a genuine smile, and the ability to not ask awkward questions. Now, our shopfront has totally evolved and transformed, and we have the ability to wow someone with a few clicks of the mouse.

Your space on the Internet is your shop window. It's the place where you can be discovered by anyone in the world, the place that says, "This is me, and this is what I do." A mistake people often make, though, is broadcasting elements of their professional life that don't need to be shared. If you have just finished a project that you did for purely financial reasons and you didn't enjoy it, then don't share it. You will attract more work based on what you choose to share, so instead list the jobs you've enjoyed and would like to do again, even if you have to include jobs you've worked on in your spare time. Get yourself in a position where your public-facing Internet presence is attracting the type of work you actually want to be doing. In short, you need to get good at PR-ing yourself.

Whom do you want to sit next to online? It's important to know who your like-minded competition is. Whom do you want to be associated with on a site like Amazon? Imagine an algorithm where they group together similar people and brands. Write a list of people whom you wouldn't mind being grouped with, and start building that network. We are more powerful when we join forces, even with those who may, in some ways, be our competitors. Whenever I am about to embark on a new project, moneymaking scheme, or fun side hustle, I look at the people already working in the space with an audience that I might like to tap into. By looking at their audience base, you can start to get a feel for whom you can target as well. Look at the Twitter accounts of those similar to you or ones that feel similar to your vibe or work and follow their followers. Cross-promote with others and collaborate to bring new visitors to both of your work. For example, collaborate with someone to make content for one another's sites and direct each other's audience to both of them.

Part of being a multi-hyphenate is selling yourself. We all have sales skills of some sort. Want to offload a piece of furniture? Want to sell spare tickets on Facebook? Want to get served first at a very busy coffee shop? In all of these scenarios, you are using natural selling skills to get what you want. Selling yourself is a daily practice in a world of online noise.

SIX WAYS TO SELL YOURSELF AND YOUR SERVICES ONLINE:

1. Have a media kit. This should include high-res logos, headshots, statistics, background information on you/your company, and testimonials.
2. Highlight any events. Are you/your business going to be popping up somewhere in real-life scenarios? If you are

hosting any events, workshops, or IRL meetups, have a separate page for this on your website.

3. Target your work! Experiment with social-media advertising by using the audience filters on Instagram or Facebook (you can target an advertisement to an audience as broad or as niche as you like, for example, 18- to 21-year-olds, those who live in New York City, those who like watching Gogglebox).

4. Be contactable. Have an email address in a *very* prominent place on your website or social media.

5. Have strong testimonials. Showcase the best things people have said about you by making them easily accessible on your website or online presence.

6. Press! If you have any press clips, post them where they'd immediately catch someone's eye.

6. YOU DON'T HAVE TO QUIT YOUR DAY JOB

It's really much better to keep a day job or at least one part-time stream of income that you are used to having. It allows you to experiment with other things without too much risk and to decide what sort of other side hustles you want to create without the added pressure of having to earn money from them immediately. (I don't get it when career books tell you to quit your job on the first page. Why would anyone advise that? "Hey, you, holding this book! Just quit your job tomorrow. Go on—just quit. It's fine!" It's not fine.)

Quitting our job in an instant is not something that a lot of us can realistically do, unless we live in a house made of gold with money trees growing in the garden. The "just go for it" mentality in many self-help books is often misplaced. You can't "reach for the stars" and "follow your dreams" with reckless abandon. Sometimes you have to wait for the right moment and create a strategy first.

However, asking for more flexibility—some unpaid time out of the office—is something you can do. It may be a sacrifice at first, losing out on paid work hours. However, the benefits can be huge: having a day to yourself to practice self-care and avoid burnout or to start building a side business that could grow and add to your income streams. Having an outside project or side hustle teaches you new skills, allows you to meet new people, and may provide you with extra income—it can empower you to make better choices in your long-term career. You want to keep your options open in an unpredictable working world. Short-term sacrifices can turn into long-term advantages. It's all about setting yourself up for the risk and having a goal in mind.

WANT TO ASK FOR FLEXIBLE WORK? HERE'S HOW I ADVISE YOU TO OFFICIALLY ASK:

» Put it in writing.
» Put a date on it.
» Describe the change you would like to make to your working schedule.
» Explain your preferred timings.
» Explain the effect that this change would have on the company.
» State whether you have made a request previously.

7. YOU'RE A MULTI-HYPHENATE, NOT A MULTITASKER

One of the biggest assumptions about being a multi-hyphenate is that you must flit between projects like a butterfly, never totally landing on one thing—which isn't at all true. You can have multiple jobs, but you still might spend more time on one than another, and if you care about what you're doing, you'll always focus on each job properly (and it's important to do just that). When you are doing one hyphen, you should totally concentrate on the task at hand. We all know that multitasking does not achieve good results.

I am a fan of the concept of "deep work," coined by Cal Newport, a professor and scientist and the author of a book on the subject, *Deep Work: Rules for Focused Success in a Distracted World*. He argues that success is all about the art of concentration and dedication and that it doesn't matter how long you work but how deeply you focus on your work. It helped me redefine what "hard work" means to me. Hard work doesn't mean working all the hours God sends you—in fact, a good in-depth thirty minutes with no distractions (no phone, no Twitter, no nothing) is actually incredibly valuable, and you can get a lot done. Author Elizabeth Gilbert famously said that she writes her novels in thirty-minute chunks each day. "Get an egg timer" is her advice for wannabe novelists. You don't need the perfect setting, a scented candle, or a cottage in the countryside; you just need thirty uninterrupted minutes. There are handy online tools like Toggl and TimeCamp that track your time and create time sheets for your business that can help spot where certain projects might be draining your time. The app Freedom blocks you from going online for eight hours, and the SelfControl app allows you to pick certain websites you want to block.

8. ACT MICRO, THINK MACRO

The Multi-Hyphen Life is not about short-term fixes but strategies and opportunities that will enable you to forge a new path that is more robust than a single-focus career.

I've realized that to feel consistently "on the pulse," I need to be part "nowist" (being good at getting lots done in a short space of time) and part "futurist" (keeping a close eye on big industry shifts). This doesn't mean knowing exactly where you'll be in five years' time (that's now impossible), but it's about looking ahead to what your chosen industries will look like in five years' time. You need to be looking at the big picture while also thinking about how you will achieve small daily successes.

We can't predict the future, but we can look at trends and try to be prepared as much as we can. Looking ahead at emerging trends, especially emerging tech trends, doesn't make you nerdy; it is absolutely crucial. One great way to do this is signing up for trend newsletters, such as trendwatching.com, or the Pocket newsletter, which sends you some of the best web-tech reads. Make a habit of curating your subscriptions and whom you follow so that you are getting useful information directly in your feed. This might mean making different Twitter lists or bookmarks or creating different personal and professional accounts. It's worth investing time in curating the outlets you read in order to get the best-quality information without having to filter through other rubbish to get to it.

9. USE YOUR ENERGY WISELY

One positive outcome of our modern tech-filled lifestyles is how personalizing our days can have a direct impact on our energy levels. We can start to unpick and figure out what fills our creative tank and what drains it. The power and control lie with us.

As technology author Tom Chatfield says: "You have limited willpower and limited mental energy." This is why the old working structure might not be working for you. Our attention spans have changed, and the way we work has changed. We need to conserve energy and use it very wisely.

Tony Schwartz, the author of *The Way We're Working Isn't Working*, says that "human beings are designed to pulse between spending energy and renewing energy."[4] Take note of what energizes you and what deflates you. Personalize your schedule. Note your energy spikes and lows. Computers can work around the clock, but we can't. It's important that we understand more about our bodies, our minds, and our own personal rhythms.

Work in units of energy and hours. I used to waste so much time when I worked in an office: cups of tea, chatting, countless pointless meetings. A workplace study found that an average working professional experiences eighty-seven interruptions per day, making it difficult to remain productive and focused for a full day.[5]

One thing I've found is that email isn't our friend. We feel productive using it, but it is a con and the biggest time suck. But we all have to use it. So here are some tips on how to tackle inbox overwhelm:

» Multiple inbox folders: For your multiple projects, have multiple email folders. Label, color-code, do whatever you need to do to get your emails out of your main inbox. Filtering them into folders means you get them out of sight and that you reply only to the messages that you absolutely need to. It also means your emails have distinctive project folders so nothing gets mixed up.

» Schedule emails: There is a difference between looking busy and being productive. Realizing I don't have to send emails in real time has changed everything for me. Sending late-night emails makes you look quite frantic, and sometimes you might want to get into someone's inbox first thing but have a meeting that clashes. I like to bulk type out my emails and then schedule them for different times depending on what's appropriate. I might reply to an email in front of the TV but schedule it for the morning. It's also a good tactic if you want to reply to an invitation but don't want to look too keen! Boomerang on Gmail is a good tool, or followup.cc, Streak, or Yesware.

» Block out solid time in your online calendar: If you want to escape constant interruptions or meetings, blocking out chunks of your planner for deep work can help stop anyone stealing away your time or your accidentally booking anything in.

10. DON'T DO STUFF FOR FREE

We've covered that whetting an appetite for your work is one part of the Multi-Hyphen Life strategy—building a micro-following, having a strong SEO and web presence, and attracting clients. But there is a difference between "putting yourself out there" to attract work and "putting your work out there, for free." Do not get into the habit of just tweeting, blogging, writing, or promoting your company or work without an end goal of what you want to sell online alongside it.

Disclaimer: I've done a lot of stuff for free in the past when it came to side hustling. When I was fresh out of university and just wanted experience, I had an entry-level job, but I also did stuff for free because in most cases I did get something in return: networking opportunities or something to add to my résumé/portfolio that had the potential to pay off tenfold later down the line. I know a lot of people whose past unpaid work at the very beginning of their careers has helped set them up for later successes.

But "exposure" just scrapes by as a payment only when you are fresh on the scene and have pretty much nothing to offer yet. The minute you have any sort of portfolio, "exposure" is laughable and should be banned from your work vocabulary. But how do we know when someone is taking us for a ride?

Most people pay handsomely for an education that is supposed to equip them for working life, only to then be faced with debts and people expecting them to work for free "for a bit" to "earn" the chance for paid work. This isn't the way it's supposed to be and is not fair at all. We need to be up front about how to make having multiple jobs a livelihood, by making sure the services we provide are paid for and paid on time. I never do anything for free unless it will allow me to reach a nonfinancial business goal. Examples of this could be an event that is full of prospective clients who will be enjoyable or a collaboration with a not-for-profit whose mission I support.

FOUR TIPS ON HOW TO MAKE SURE YOU GET PAID FOR YOUR WORK

1. Get a middleman or middlewoman: It's often worth hiring someone to sit in between you and the client who can invoice and chase the payments (like a virtual PA). You then get to stick to the bit you're good at—doing the work!—and avoid getting bogged down in admin.

2. Automation: Services like Zervant allow you to set up recurring invoices to retained clients so you don't have to worry about doing the same repetitive paperwork every month.

3. Be upfront at the beginning. Make sure your payment policy (how many days, etc.) is clear and in writing. If you can, ask for 50 percent of the money upfront before you begin the work. Be clear about the parameters of the project and that any extra work would need to be invoiced separately. Also, sometimes it's good to ask about their payment system/process beforehand, just so you know.

4. Don't be afraid to ask for more: You're allowed to ask anything! The answer is never personal, just practical. And make sure you raise your rates as you gain experience. You might not be working in a traditional company, but you should review, promote yourself, and give yourself a pay raise when you've earned it! (You'll find more tips on money in chapter 10.)

»»»

Refer back to this tool kit whenever you feel as though you need a push to bring some of your new ideas to life. The Multi-Hyphen Life is all about reinventing yourself and your career and staying nimble, but it's important to (a) remember why you're doing it and (b) pinpoint the basic foundations you already have in place so you can repeat your success each time.

Chapter 8

THE FOUR FS: FAILURE, FAIRNESS, FLEXIBILITY, FEELINGS

When I set out to write about changing work culture, I realized four themes kept coming up. These were: straight up messing up, the confidence gap, the challenge of asking for flexibility, and how our emotions affect our work and work decisions. I sorted these into the four Fs: Failure, Feminism, Flexibility, and Feelings.

This isn't a book just for women, but when talking about success, it's hard not to take into account how much the confident alpha approach seems to be rewarded and ingrained in our work culture, and that is often something men already have a leg up on. A patriarchal society affects both men and women; men's setbacks in the workplace are a feminist issue too. Paternity leave is important for men, yet many workplaces still don't see it as something they should give out generously. And research by men's mental health charity the Campaign against Living Miserably (CALM) and the Huffington Post UK found that 87 percent of men wish they could spend more time with their children. "Bro" culture can be toxic for both men and women. Equality in the workplace will be a win for us all.

Failure and Fear

I couldn't write a book about work and personal success and not include a chapter on failure. I personally find failure a bit fetishized in business books and "progressive" work cultures. Samuel Beckett quotes (like "Try again. Fail again. Fail better.") are plastered all over start-up offices. Failure can be important for the life lessons you learn from it, but it's also not fun, at all.

But, of course, we all face failure and setbacks along the way, no matter what our job is. It's no different for multi-hyphenates, and as much as I wanted to write about the highs, I couldn't ignore the lows. Perhaps you're reading this and don't feel like you have a support system when it comes to your career and decision-making. Maybe you're in lots of private Facebook groups but are too scared to write in them because the community feels slightly intimidating. Maybe you feel like you can't ask your parents for advice because they have a perception of work and success different from yours. Maybe you have just made a big career change and worry about the future. Setbacks and obstacles in work (and life in general) aren't specific to one industry. Feeling like you're treading water, feeling like you're comparing yourself with the person next to you, and feeling like you're not using your full potential are the same old issues people have always battled with over the course of their working lives. The same work insecurities affect us all, no matter our background, age, or position on the career ladder. Crisis in confidence, especially at work, happens to everyone.

Every job, project, promotion, or big task creates a fear of failing. This doesn't magically go away when you live a multi-hyphenate lifestyle. Every job brings along its own challenges. When I interviewed the author and popular poet Laura Dockrill, she said she often worries that by having multiple different projects, she'll never end up having "one full glass of milk," just lots of half glasses. Author Caroline O'Donoghue says, "I get the vibe off people that I'm sort of a grappling millennial upstart, jack-of-all-trades-ing it because I'm not really good enough to do one thing well."

Facebook claims it's created over 4.5 million jobs.[1] Facebook has only eight thousand employees, so what they mean is jobs have been created off the back of their business, for example: social-media marketers, developers, manufacturers of Internet equipment. Some people might roll their eyes at these new job titles. But these new roles have quickly integrated themselves into traditional workforces. Soon it will be hard to remember how we went about things without them—a bit like how computers replaced paperwork.

People love to mock new ways of working. But accepting that people might turn their nose up at your career choices is a small price to pay when you think of how far ahead you will be in the long run.

I definitely mark down my own struggles with fear and failure as learning experiences. I let stigma get to me for years before taking on this lifestyle. I had been starting to earn good money from my side projects (a thriving blog, consultancy via Skype, speaking engagements at conferences and panels all over the world), but other people's opinions of what "success" and a "proper job" were really held me back from managing my projects on my own terms. I still felt like I needed to work for a "proper company" and have a job title that meant something to outsiders. I was elated when a panel event I did first introduced me by talking about my side projects, not my job title or company affiliation. They didn't care where my full-time job was; that wasn't the reason I was there.

I remember drawing a little red dot in the corner of my paper planner every time I felt like my side projects could earn the same amount of money outside of the office as I could in it. I finished the year with 320 red dots. It was only then that I was brave enough to leave my job. I definitely don't recommend rash decisions, but if we have something that is working, or starting to work, and we have enough of a safety net, we should be encouraged to try something new.

Another example of fear is the mid- or quarter-life crisis. We hit a wall, feeling utterly miserable, and think, *Is this really it?* Millennials, especially millennial women, are more likely to experience a quarter-life crisis. In a piece published in the Cut called "The Ambition Collision," Lisa Miller wrote: "Women enter workplaces filled with ambition and optimism and then, by 30 or so, become wise to the ways in which they are stuck."[2] Many of us bought into the idea of "having it all" or "the dream job," and the reality that such things may not really exist is a hard pill to swallow. That feeling is scary no matter what age you are—realizing that, actually, there's no pot of gold at the end of the rainbow. This is it. This is just how life is going to be. Miller continued, "It's as if the women have cleared spaces in their lives for meteoric careers, and then those careers have been less gratifying, or harder won, or more shrunken than they'd imagined. And what's there to fill the space, except more Insta images of female gratification—vacations! cocktails!—that inadequately reflect the lives they lead?"

I definitely related to this. You can have all of the "on-paper" successes—a good salary, a great Instagram feed, and nice material objects—but you realize soon enough that it can leave you feeling strangely empty.

When I first told people I was writing a book about the Multi-Hyphen Life, a few eyebrows raised around me. Some of the responses I got included: "But the gig economy is a bad thing!" "Are you teaching people how to be an influencer?" and "That sounds like more work." Of course, that's not what this book is about, but it shows how resistant people are to new ways of doing things. Everyone has an opinion on the #FutureOfWork. Every day a new invention pops up, every day a new "solution" to our ever-growing digital problems, and yet we have systems in place for working that were invented for a different (Victorian) century. The workplace has been s-l-o-w to change.

The current school system is out-of-date when it comes to the modern workplace. We should be learning about digital privacy, security, social-media etiquette, public shaming, the new job market, starting your own business, and mental health tools. If self-employment is on the rise as a whole, then we should teach people about how to save and invest money and how to do taxes. We should teach young people how to keep themselves relevant, curious, and interested. Of course, this is not yet the way the world works. And when we find that the working world has not caught up to our changing needs, it's no surprise that fear, failure, and life crises follow.

Fairness and the Confidence Gap

"Success, it turns out, correlates just as closely with confidence as it does with competence. No wonder that women, despite all our progress, are still woefully underrepresented at the highest levels. All of that is the bad news. The good news is that with work, confidence can be acquired. Which means that the confidence gap, in turn, can be closed."

—KATTY KAY and CLAIRE SHIPMAN,
"The Confidence Gap," the *Atlantic*[3]

The confidence gap is a big talking point in terms of getting what we want in the workplace. Most people—but women in particular—struggle with advocating for what they want. The world is a scary place, and it never feels like there's a good time to take any risks. However, that's the only way to make a change (whether it's a high- or low-level risk). In order to make a change, you have to take that scary first step. When I asked on Twitter, "Say you have a project or side hustle you've been meaning to start for ages, what are the roadblocks you are facing?" the answers were nearly all about confidence, or lack thereof:

> » "Tragic levels of self-confidence, low funds, little knowledge (or few people to ask for advice) and bad management of time."
> » "Self-belief/imposter syndrome."
> » "Fear of failing, prioritizing, self-doubt."
> » "Self-belief and feeling that it's 'been done.'"
> » "Confidence to actually do it; often it's a lovely concept, but making it a reality is a much bigger scarier step."

Another: "Lack of knowledge about where to start—like trying to dive without any water!" And another: "Lack of confidence, self-loathing."

There were some other reasons in there—money, as well as lack of energy, time, and resources—but I was really taken aback by the overwhelming confidence crises most people expressed.

It's really important that we talk about this, because confidence to take risks and take things into your own hands will play a bigger role as work continues to change. As executive career coach Gwendolyn Parkin says, "The employer or industry will no longer be the center of your career—you will be." As more people become consultants and self-employed and we navigate future jobs that haven't been invented yet, more people will be at the center of their career decisions.

And while many men and women lack confidence in the workplace, there are marked gender iniquities. In the United Kingdom, research from monster.co.uk in conjunction with YouGov revealed that there is a career crisis among young female workers, with 71 percent saying they lack confidence in asking for a pay raise. And men have more self-confidence about technology than women, with 43 percent of women describing their computing skills as "good enough" compared with 35 percent of men.[4]

Countless studies show similar disparities. Reasons for this vary, from lack of representation in leadership roles, leading to fewer role models and mentors, to negative competition as women are pitted against one another for the few female "spots" at the top. From my experience in the workplace, I am sad to say I still feel the competitiveness in the air, often from other women in my field. I wish it wasn't the case—it feels like a hangover from the past.

Confidence can't be bought or sold, but we can take measures to try to encourage more risk taking and a little more bravery to try something new.

FIVE THINGS I LIKE TO REMIND MYSELF ABOUT CONFIDENCE

1. Most people are checking their own online profiles out more than yours. Most people are thinking about themselves most of the time. No one is looking that closely at you.

2. Confidence comes from practicing things over and over again. There's no quick and easy fix; keep repeating and learning.

3. Make an inbox folder called "Nice things" and put complimentary emails in there. Anytime you get imposter syndrome, you can refer back to this folder, which helps remind you that you know what you're doing.

4. Say yes to things that scare you and know it will make things easier in the long run.

5. Nerves look and feel very similar to excitement. If you're nervous, try to change this feeling into excitement; more confidence will follow.

6. Confidence can be quiet and subtle. It doesn't always carry a loud, booming voice or wear a power suit.

The Dirty F Word: Flexibility

Flexible working is the future. A little bit of flex would go a really long way toward making the workplace more equitable. A study by the Equality and Human Rights Commission estimates that approximately fifty-four thousand new mothers lose their jobs across the United Kingdom every year—almost twice the number identified in similar research in 2005.[5] It also unearthed that 10 percent of women were put off from attending postnatal appointments by their bosses, putting their health and the health of their babies at risk.

According to workingfamilies.org (the United Kingdom's leading work-life balance organization): "Any employee (other than an employee shareholder) with 26 weeks of service with the same employer has the right to make a request to work flexibly; you don't have to be a parent and carer."[6] It's assumed that flexibility is a priority for mostly mothers, but it's something that fathers want too. According to the Pew Research Center, 48 percent of working fathers say a flexible work schedule is extremely valuable to them.[7]

Being a multi-hyphenate is synonymous with wanting flexibility in your career. You want to work on different projects, regardless of whether you are a parent. You might want a day or afternoon off to add in a new hyphen, be it spending time with your child or wanting to paint alone by the sea. So how do you actually go about asking for that?

I wanted to ask Karen Mattison, MBE, cofounder and joint CEO of Timewise, her thoughts. In 2016, she put the issue of flexible hiring—flexible working from day one—on the wider agenda with the launch of Hire Me My Way, a national campaign in the United Kingdom funded by the Big Lottery Fund to grow the flexible-jobs market. Five years ago, she launched the Power Part Time List in the *Financial Times*, a roll call of fifty men and women who work in senior roles on less than five full days a week. I asked her about why people still defend the rigid structure of the workplace despite the hard evidence against its efficiency:

Emma: So why are people still embarrassed by asking for or having flexibility in their careers?

Karen: Flexible working can often be seen as "dirty," as it is assumed to be good for employees and bad for business—which, as we know, is simply not true. Flexible working, and in particular part-time working, has long been hampered by a negative branding, not least in the context of senior part-time working. Because when it comes to the top team, businesses often look for nothing less than total commitment, and they often—not always—believe the best measure of that is the number of hours an executive spends in the office, rather than focus on delivery.

Emma: It appears that this old trope of hours done equaling success hasn't really gone away much.

Karen: From a personal perspective, after struggling in the jobs market myself as a parent, I have devoted the last fifteen years of my career to driving change and helping more women work flexibly—in part-time roles or flexible shift patterns or through working from home. But when I first started on this journey, the world of work was a different place. Now, it is time to take a step back and think again, as the world of work already has changed, and how people work has changed. It's business that needs to catch up.

Emma: It's an interesting point, that people have changed very quickly—the way we live, buy, consume, meet up, eat, travel, date—and it's the businesses that have had to adapt for new needs. And what about the old stigma of flexible working also being something just for parents?

Karen: I believe that the focus on "making work, work" for women with children, paradoxically, may no longer be the right thing for women. When it comes to the issue of flexible working, for too long it has been viewed as a concession—given to those who somehow can't work in a "normal" way. When, in fact, if we look at the cold, hard evidence, there are two critical points. First, flexible working is not just good for mothers. It has been proved to be hugely beneficial to businesses—from improving staff productivity, attraction, and retention, as well as reducing travel and property costs. Second, if we take a wide definition of flexible working—where, when, and how much people work—we see that it is not purely the working pattern of choice for women with children. The demand cuts across all ages and genders, across all life stages, and for a whole host of reasons. We need to think again. Flexibility is not for the marginalized; it's for the many.

Flexible working shouldn't be seen as a privilege; it should be a worker's right. I also spoke to Rachel Mostyn from the Digital Mums group, the founders of #WorkThatWorks, for her thoughts on why people can be quite reluctant to embrace the idea that flexibility could be a perk for everyone. She said:

"I think it's human nature to be scared of change. And I get that. We are an extreme example of a flexible working business, with 100 percent of our team able to work remotely and flexibly. We understand, though, that you can't just go fully flexible overnight, so what we suggest instead is that businesses dip a toe in the water and see how they might be able to introduce flexible-working policies than can benefit both them and their employees—for example, trialing one team working flexible hours for a week or another team working from a different location. If you measure on output vs. presenteeism [the practice of being present at one's place of work for more hours than is required], I'm confident you'll notice no difference and will in fact see a bigger uplift in productivity. I also think too many businesses still believe that if you can see your employee at a desk, then they must be working. My answer to this is always that if you can't trust your employees to work when you can't see them, then you have a bigger issue than flexible working!"

In a piece for *Campaign* magazine Christina Lemieux (global planning director at ad agency Leo Burnett) wrote: "The word 'part-timer' has traditionally been used in a negative way to call out someone for not being fully committed to their job. Speaking as a dedicated part-time worker (and one of the UK's top 50 power part-timers), I'd argue it is time to move on from that perception and appreciate that the support of part-time and flexible working in this industry is not only important, but the way forward."[8] It's true: perceptions need to change. There is still a stigma to working part-time, even if it means working the exact same amount, just across multiple disciplines or jobs.

Subtle comments can take their toll and also point to the old-fashioned ingrained ways of thinking. Writer Sirena Bergman said in a series of tweets: "I hate when people casually ask 'oh are you working today?' as though being self-employed = being a student or something / Were YOU working today or did you spend most of your morning scrolling through BuzzFeed and then go to the pub for 2 hours at lunch?" A *GQ* article written by Jonathan Heaf approached the idea of a multi-hyphenate with a, shall we say, mocking tone: "On my last trip to LA, I was introduced to a freelance noise architect/nutritional strategist/sand artist. As far as I can work out, none of these things are real jobs—or they certainly shouldn't be."[9]

Whenever I do company events about multi-hyphenate careers or the future of work, there will always be someone who will come up to me at the end, looking a little deflated. The questions are always around the setbacks they are experiencing: Their parents don't support the decision; they're struggling to balance a full-time job with a side project; they have money worries; they don't know whether they have a good idea. What's interesting is sometimes I hardly have to say anything. I listen while they speak at length about their idea, their plan, their resources. And, usually, it's all there. They aren't really asking for advice; they are instead looking for reassurance or a nod of approval. It's interesting to observe, and it highlights the confidence gap so many of us struggle with.

We all want approval. When I asked Vicki, a thirty-two-year-old PR consultant, about what spurs her on, she said: "I know it's sad that I need to be recognized by others, but it's not just my boss telling me I'm doing a good job; it's my friends and family saying they're proud of me or admiring a cool project that I'm working on." I don't think that's sad at all. It's human nature to want our parents and friends to be proud of us and tell us we are doing a good job. We need more conversations and resources to address these very human feelings.

Another myth of working flexibly is the romanticization of "being our own boss!!!" Almost no one is solely their own boss, especially if you live the multi-hyphenate lifestyle. Yes, you can design your own schedule. Yes, you decide what projects you want to take on. However, you still have bosses! You still have good and bad bosses! The very nature of having clients means that bosses are still a part of your life. That is the nature of work. It's important we stop promoting the #BeYourOwnBoss mantra. By definition, work means you often do things you don't want to do with people you don't necessarily want to work with.

The Multi-Hyphen Life offers respite from traditional, artificially lit office life. But it is not to be confused with the #goals captions you see being perpetuated on Instagram. We have a tendency to see a nicely lit photo of something online and project a utopian fantasy onto it. "Desk porn" is real. Instagram "workspace porn" is growing. Instead of romanticizing "being your own boss," I think you should focus on setting up your own ecosystem that allows you maximum flexibility and control. The freelance life is far from perfect. But having a myriad of different careers that you merge and make work for you is, I think, one of the best options out there right now for a work-life balance.

You've got this.

Q&A with Anna Whitehouse, founder of the #FlexAppeal movement

I spoke to Anna Whitehouse, a writer-blogger-podcaster-campaigner-author-founder of the parenting media hub Mother Pukka, and asked her about her campaign, #FlexAppeal. She believes people should have flexibility in their lives in order to reach their full potential in their personal and professional realms.

Emma: What was your biggest disappointment when it came to the workplace? What had to change?

Anna: The moment when I realized my employers were not looking at what we were doing but simply where we were sitting. That was when I mentally quit. It seems obvious as an employer that you would focus on output over simply chastising someone for being in at 9:02 a.m.

Emma: What are the biggest challenges you've faced in your #FlexAppeal campaign?

Anna: People thinking it doesn't affect them. The assumption that it's a "mummy wants to see more of her Weetabix-smattered child" issue. Flexible working is for everyone. We are no longer a generation that simply seeks things (holidays, fat salaries, benefits); we also seek life. We seek a work-life balance, and the companies that get that will attract the talent.

Emma: Also, what do you say to naysayer people who say flexibility is bad because it means you could work 24-7 on your phone from anywhere?

Anna: It's about control. It's about controlling how and where you work to the best of your ability. Everyone will do this differently, and some will not thrive in this environment. But, then, many don't thrive in the archaic nine-to-five system. I've stopped pretending I'm not a mother at work, and I've stopped pretending I'm not working when at home. I am happier and healthier, and in combining those two things I'm able to give more to my job. I wrote a *Sunday Times* bestselling book in two months while pregnant and without wanting to be a praise monkey; I want that to be living proof to my previous employers of what can be achieved with a little flex.

Emma: Where do you think the workplace is heading?

Anna: In this digitally savvy world it has to be moving to a more flexible realm. It was Sir Ian McKellen's great-great-grandfather who pioneered the two-day weekend in the 1800s. That's working out OK for us all. It's simply a matter of time.

Feelings and Work Emotion

In Shakespeare, Julius Caesar famously wept at the feet of a statue of Alexander the Great: "Do you not think it is matter for sorrow that while Alexander, at my age, was already king of so many peoples, I have as yet achieved no brilliant success?"[10]

People have always compared themselves with others (even Caesar!). But before the Internet, at least we weren't tuned into other people's every passing thought or life #goals 24-7. We are constantly exposed to other people's digitally curated perfect lives. The onslaught of images makes it hard for us to be happy with what we've got. How do we make sure we are looking after our mental health and not comparing ourselves all the time?

A friend of mine, Lucy Sheridan, is the United Kingdom's first ever comparison coach. She guides and coaches people and businesses on how to live comparison-free or at least how to turn down the volume on your inner critic and nosy neighbor. One of my favorite sayings of hers is "Don't be somebody else's tribute act." She also describes Instagram as the "Las Vegas of comparison." It's such a good description—the Internet really is full of bright lights and loud music and artifice that make you think that everyone else is having a better time on planet Earth than you.

Here's my theory: It's harder to compare yourself with others when you are owning your own path, your own setup, your own hyphens. It's harder to compare when your work life looks different from other people's. It's harder to compare when there's not one single idea of success or one ladder for all. Rather than comparing yourself with others, allow yourself to be inspired by and learn from them.

Working for yourself or on your own projects can often be a lonely experience at times. It can come as a shock if you are used to being surrounded by noisy colleagues in a noisy office space. As author Steven Heighton says, "Now, social media and the internet offer the introvert a poisonous compromise: you can be alone in your room and at the same time connected to others, if more or less on your own terms. Alone, yet not alone."[11]

It's a serious discussion, considering that Gen Z have grown up in a world where they don't have to leave the house because they can do everything from their laptops. In a piece in the *Atlantic*, psychologist Jean M. Twenge wrote, "Social-networking sites like Facebook promise to connect us to friends. But the portrait of iGen teens emerging from the data is one of a lonely, dislocated generation."[12] It's a real concern. We should make sure we are making real connections and maintaining real relationships.

It's one thing opening up your work life to more flexibility and having a little bit of flex here and there, but this isn't about totally turning your back on some traditional aspects of work like connecting with colleagues. Flexibility can mean prioritizing friends, self-care, family life, having enough time off to avoid burnout, having the occasional afternoon off, or a job share so you have more time for side hustles or simply being there at school pickup. These are all positive things and can dramatically change a lifestyle. However, it's all about balance. An article in *Harvard Business Review* said: "In the workplace, new models of working—such as telecommuting and some on-demand 'gig economy' contracting arrangements—have created flexibility but often reduce the opportunities for in-person interaction and relationships."[13] I want to emphasize the importance of IRL contact. One of the biggest myths is that as a multi-hyphenate, especially when your hyphens are in the digital sphere, you spend all your time online or on your own. Being flexible doesn't have to mean spending all your time solo. It's important to keep up connections that you would otherwise make and maintain by physically being in the office.

Author and freelance writer Morgan Jerkins wrote on Twitter: "Mon-Fri, if I'm not going out to eat with someone, I may only speak a sentence or two to a delivery guy or fitness instructor. I realized this when I started teaching online. My jaw would start hurting and I was like, 'Whoa, when's the last time I actually spoke?'" I am grateful for people like Morgan for sharing their honest experiences of how they struggle to keep things balanced. This kind of reality check helps us all learn and grow and maybe be more mindful about our own choices.

I find social media the best way to meet like-minded people—people with whom to share a real-life coffee! Michelle Kennedy launched the Peanut app for moms who want to connect, whether that's messaging while at home breastfeeding or meeting up in person. In my own life, Twitter, private Facebook groups, and Instagram have all facilitated my meeting up with people. (It helps that my job is to interview people, too.) It's important not to let "remote working" mean "too much time alone." Tech has allowed us to earn money online, but we still need face-to-face interactions and opportunities to meet new people.

HOW TO BE SOCIAL OUTSIDE OF TRADITIONAL OFFICE SPACES

» Book a breakfast meeting first thing so that you start off your day with an IRL connection.
» Join a monthly book club so that you regularly meet new people in an enjoyable safe space.
» Sign up for Eventbrite alerts for events or networking opportunities local to you on themes that interest you.
» Have a set time in the week dedicated to meetings where you can meet everyone in one go. Try not to agree to coffees sprinkled throughout the day, as this can limit how much time you can work uninterrupted on other projects. Remember that traveling to meetings can burn through a lot of time too; try to use that time wisely while commuting.
» Have your own happy hours with other multi-hyphenate friends (same for holiday parties).

No job or working life is perfect. It would be naive to assume there is a one-size-fits-all solution that works for everyone. Any lifestyle takes maintenance, motivation, and conquering obstacles—dealing with the four Fs as they relate to you. But the benefits of facing these issues head-on and advocating for freedom and autonomy can definitely outweigh the negatives.

Chapter 9

REAL VS. SHALLOW CONNECTIONS

"You have to build your own networks, make friends with people, cross benches, friends on the left, right and middle. It involves lots of cups of tea—no magic. I'm building networks so hopefully when you need them in future you can ask for their support."

—MARTHA LANE FOX, founder of LastMinute.com

A crucial aspect of creating your own career is knowing how to socialize and build connections in a way that works for you. Not everyone is comfortable metaphorically singing and jazz-hands-ing their way through networking events. In fact, I don't know anyone who enjoys talking to strangers while wearing a name tag and holding a glass of slightly warm wine. It's easy to let social anxiety take over, and it's very hard to be yourself in such contrived scenarios.

However, there's no denying that networking is important. Connecting with new people (online and IRL) means that the chances of your being seen and potentially employed or commissioned increase. Putting a face to an email address and meeting people in person are so important; meeting a lot of new people regularly and getting out of your same circle are important. How probable is it that you will get that job/project/deal? The probability lies in how much you are willing to put yourself out there, put yourself in different rooms, and reach out and connect with others. It's a numbers game.

"What do you do?" is one of the first things people ask to get a sense of who you are, even though it's often not the best question to ask to truly get to know someone. There are better leading questions to ask. Each of these questions below allows someone to mention their day job, side hustle, or simply what they enjoy doing with their time without directly asking them "What do you do for a job?" And, yes, I crowdsourced these on Twitter.

THINGS TO ASK INSTEAD OF "SO, WHAT DO YOU DO?"
» What are you excited about at the moment?
» What are you working on right now?
» What do you like to do?
» How can I check out your work?
» What brings you to this event?
» What's your latest obsession?
» What have you done recently that you're most proud of?
» What are you passionate about?
» What do you do for fun?

It's Not Whom You Know, It's Who Knows You

The goal is for people to know you, know of you, know of your work. This isn't an exercise in "getting famous on the Internet" (that is definitely not the answer), but the more people know of what you (or your company) do, the better. It's about being recognized by people who might go on to tell others about you and your work. It's exactly the same as having a local business in a tiny town where everyone knows of you. You would want people to know the sign above your door and tell their friends to come to your shop or local business. It's taking that small-town, trusted approach and applying it to the Internet.

TIPS FOR CONNECTING ONLINE

» Back in the day, people would have a little black book of all their contacts; now we have digital tools. Google Sheets can be a good place to write down names and companies to keep track of people you've met. Twitter lists are useful for different categories of contacts.

» Follow up soon after you've met in person. Strike while the iron is hot.

» Try not to breadcrumb (the act of leading someone on by contacting them intermittently—be that by text or email or social media—to keep them hanging on). Be up front about whether or not you have time to meet up. It makes it easier when both parties are honest about their schedules instead of wasting time going back and forth.

» Don't be too overfamiliar—you're not in best friend territory yet.

» Follow new people regularly. To find new people to follow, who you think might like your work or company, find a similar company/person whom you like and see who follows them.

» Be open-minded. Try new apps (business apps like Bumble Bizz have launched to rival LinkedIn). If they work for you, great! But if they don't work for you, don't force it. Experiment and find the platforms that best suit you.

» It's not about the follower count when it comes to having a good, strong network. Having lots of online followers doesn't necessarily mean you have a larger network. Put in the time to grow and nurture microcommunities—in private groups, email threads, or regular meet-ups.

» Get in touch with people only when it's truly relevant for both of you. The aim with networking and connecting is to make everyone's lives easier. Make a mutually beneficial suggestion. Be targeted in everything you do.

» Don't make a habit of straight up asking people you hardly know for favors. Make an effort to make it worth their while.

And remember: There's nothing worse than the phrase "Can I pick your brain?"

» Connect and introduce other people in your network to each other. Do it without an agenda, but those two people will remember you for connecting them. (This can also be done IRL!)

Why You Need to Get Offline to Meet People

"I am telling you that the longer you look into that magical window in your phone, the farther you will drift from the heart of who you are."

—HEATHER HAVRILESKY, the Cut's "Ask Polly"

Networking online can bring you lots of opportunities and connections. Sometimes a gem of an email falls into your inbox because of your name popping up time and time again. Sometimes you do get a magic "follow" on Twitter that leads to a huge piece of work. But Twitter, Instagram, and LinkedIn are also full of nonopportunities, spammy messages, and dead connections. It's worth being aware that although using social media can help build your network, it's not everything when it comes to making solid, long-term connections with people. True connection takes time and long-term investment. There's nothing wrong with building up your "numbers," but sitting in your bedroom liking, commenting, and following people doesn't necessarily build lasting relationships. That is not a long-term career strategy. "Connecting" behind a screen will never be as powerful as connecting in real life. In order to truly connect, you have to get out there, in the real world, meeting people face-to-face.

One of the biggest myths I'd like to dispel is that people need to sit behind their laptops "networking" their way through Twitter lists, using bots and apps and buttons. That's wrong on many levels, but it's mainly wrong to think you can make strong connections by simply pressing "like" or posting a handful of comments. Any publicist knows the first rule is to put a face to a name to start to build up a real relationship and to pitch things that would genuinely appeal to the recipient. People you barely know who make big asks via an out-of- the-blue email don't seem to understand why that will never work. With so many demands on our time already, it's hard to justify spending it doing big favors for strangers. Good work is built on trust, and it's natural to want to work with those we have true connections with over someone we don't know too well. This chapter offers practical advice on how to build meaningful life- and work-enhancing relationships. I don't believe in quick fixes when it comes to building a network.

IRL NETWORKING DOS AND DON'TS
DO

» Be nice. It is underrated. Some people think that being aloof seems powerful and mysterious, but really it reads as cold.

» As author Caitlin Moran says, "Just resolve to shine, constantly and steadily, like a warm lamp in the corner, and people will want to move towards you in order to feel happy."[1] People are attracted to other people who make them feel good, not intimidated.

» Memorize your elevator pitch that sums up what you do in a way that isn't long-winded or too brief. Try not to sound too rehearsed. Be honest. When you ask someone a question, really listen to their response. Don't dart your eyes around the room looking for someone else. Jessica Hagy, author of *How to Be Interesting,* says, "If you let other people open up and talk about themselves, you become memorable."[2]

» Organize your own event. You will meet new people, but you will be in control of the plans for the evening.

» Bring a friend who is happy to tag along and be your networking wingperson. Help them out in return.

» Carry simple and clear business cards. As much as people think print is dead, it's not yet. People still use business cards. Even a simple card with just your email on it is easier than asking someone to take down your info on the fly. I love getting home and going through all the cards I've collected in my pocket. (My editor said she was given a business card years ago with a picture of the person as a child, on a horse, looking grumpy. It worked, as she remembers it, even now!)

» Trust your gut. We each read and take on board someone's energy consciously and subconsciously. It's OK if you don't gel with someone.

DON'T

» Don't drag on a conversation for longer than it needs to be, whether you connect really well or not at all. Feel free to move around the room. If you need to exit the conversation politely, you can introduce them to someone else and slip away; ask for a business card or contact details, which naturally rounds off the conversation; or go and get a drink or food!

» Don't drink too much. (Note to self.)

» Don't say you'll email someone or that you'll be in touch if you're not going to. Take a business card anyway, though.

» Don't pitch yourself straightaway even if you feel tempted to. Build a rapport first.

It's Not Always About You

The nature of social media means that we are free to broadcast our lives to others. We talk about ourselves a lot more than we used to. Part of being your own mini media house is having a personal online strategy and mastering your social-media etiquette. However, to truly connect, we can't be shouting about ourselves the whole time. Behaviorist and author Vanessa Van Edwards says that there are many different types of people in social situations, one of which are "conversational narcissists"—these are people who hog the conversation and make it all about them. I bet you know someone who fits this mold, who doesn't let you get a word in edgeways. Well, don't be one of these people online either.

Why You Should Quit Hate-Following

Hate-following is a very easy trap to fall into. It's when you follow an account (Instagram, website, Twitter feed, blog), even though for some reason it enrages you or makes you stew. Maybe you justify following because it's educational to read opinions you disagree with (even if they are harmful or make you feel bad), or you feel must keep up for work purposes, or any number of excuses. But if an account's content regularly leaves you with negative feelings, you might be hate-following.

Some hate-follows are harmless in the short term but over time can leave you feeling angrier, less motivated, less inspired. It's time for us to take control of our online environments just like we would with our offline ones. I wouldn't walk into a pub with someone waving a knife outside it, so why would I wander into a hate-forum that hosts horrible people? Every time we open the Internet, we are strapping ourselves in for an unknown ride. We don't know what we are going to see—you don't have to hate-follow anyone to accidentally stumble upon nastiness—but the best way to look after our mental health and feel more in control is to make sure our feeds are curated to a certain extent. We should make sure that we are following each person or account with intention and for the right reasons. Be conscious of whether you're wasting your time on things that don't inspire you or have any purpose in terms of connection. Stop hate-following.

Monitor how you feel after you've been on social media. Rate your mood out of ten. If you want to improve your mood, think about the accounts you follow and which ones might be a secret hate-follow. See whether your mood improves over time, experimenting with whom you follow and unfollow.

HOW DO YOU KNOW WHETHER SOMEONE IS A HATE-FOLLOW?

» You find yourself looking up their page when you're feeling like you need to vent.

» You roll your eyes or feel deflated when you see their images but still find yourself scrolling through them.

» You would actively avoid them in real life.

Beware of "Bubbles"

Another reason that IRL connections are so important is because they allow interactions to happen without the help of an algorithm. At networking events we are able to meet people at random. Random encounters are a bit less random on the Internet because any sort of "discover" tab on Instagram or other social app has been tailored to us based on our previous likes or follows. As Managing Director of the Webby Awards Claire Graves put it, quite rightly, "Technology changes the way people interact with each other, and some serendipity is lost along the way."[3] This is not a revelation, but it is still really relevant. Our search results, our clicks, and our swipes are not entirely random. My search page will look different from yours, even if we search for the exact same thing—Google tailors your results based on your past searches and activity. We are not seeing things as organically as we think. Our search engines and feeds are full of ads and sponsored posts and a whole load of behind-the-scenes formulas that adapt to what they think we want to see. It's important to sometimes get out of our Internet bubble to find new, exciting work and connections. For this reason it is crucial that we get offline to meet people out of our immediate online circles and broaden our horizons. It's important that we get out of our online bubble so that we can attract some work opportunities to add to our multi-hyphenate work streams. The success of a multi-hyphenate life is dependent on your solid network and on having authentic connections with lots of different people.

SIX WAYS TO GET OUT OF YOUR FILTER BUBBLE

1. Balance your news intake; follow a range of different outlets. Curation websites like AllSides.com try to give you an unbiased look across the spectrum of news outlets.
2. Follow a few newsletters that include article roundups. You will benefit from their legwork.
3. Sites like StumbleUpon allow you to, funnily enough, stumble upon different articles and bits of inspiration.
4. Be aware of algorithms that might hide your favorite social-media profiles. Make your own lists to check.
5. Go to events with friends from different industries. Got a friend with a totally different job from yours? Go with them to one of their work events as their guest and vice versa. It might be a good way to meet new people and tell them about what you do.
6. Attend a nontraditional networking event, maybe one where you connect with others over a meal or activity. They're not all happy hours.

How to Turn Your Digital Acquaintances into a Sustainable IRL Support Network

Networking is not about meeting one person who might change your life. It's not like Emma Stone singing "Someone in the Crowd" in *La La Land*. It's about making lots of genuine connections over time, having many people root for you while you root for them in return, celebrating others, and building trusted relationships in the industry you move in. Writer Ann Friedman coined the phrase "kissing sideways" to describe successful networking (as opposed to "kissing up"). She said "the idea that you need an established, well-known person is not always the case. This concept of 'kissing sideways' is making a good cohort of colleagues and support [networks] instead of finding one person to bring you up with them."[4] Networking is one of the most important aspects of being a multi-hyphenate. Yes, having a good personal brand is important, but a good personal brand means nothing if you don't have good relationships with people.

HOW TO MAINTAIN YOUR NETWORK

» Start a casual WhatsApp group, Facebook group, or Slack channel for some of your digital acquaintances who share a common thread or interest. Use it as a way to dip in and out and use it as a judgment-free zone, a place to talk fees, projects, goals.

» Ask questions and open up opportunities for others to ask you questions too. Even if you don't see someone in person that often, you can still build a mutually beneficial relationship via messaging apps.

» Whenever the opportunity arises to get someone else hired on a project, let your network know. Share job postings, project work, and assignments freely.

» Never close off new additions to the network or collective; avoid building a clique.

» Big-up your community online. Use the premise behind Follow Friday and celebrate your favorite contacts online often across social media.

» Set realistic goals regarding your meetups. Maybe they're monthly, maybe quarterly.

» Something doesn't always have to be about work for it to be a good work opportunity. Joining a book club or going to social events can be just as fun and "networky."

» Make sure you are efficient with your meetups. Never book a coffee in the middle of the day at a place that will take you ages to get to.

Aim for That Instant "I Get What You're About" Moment

I honestly believe that a lot of my success has been driven by my ability to connect instantly and sell what I'm about. I've had some incredibly high-profile names on my podcast, but why would they want to come on my show? When I approached tech mogul Seth Godin (one of the biggest marketers in the United States), I knew I had to very clearly achieve the following in a short and simple way: (a) prove why my show was worth going on, (b) explain who I am, and (c) ensure he knew exactly what to expect.

I knew I had to pitch it wisely. Rather than just pitching the strongest qualities about me and the show, I tailored my pitch by thinking about what would make me unique and interesting if I were Seth Godin receiving my unsolicited email. I think it helps to try to put yourself in someone else's shoes in that moment. If you were them, what would make you say yes? You have to have conviction in your pitch. Mine revolved around how by coming on my podcast, he could reach a new-to-him audience of mostly young women in their twenties and thirties. I knew I had to give a unique spin on it; otherwise, why would he do it?

Seth didn't know who I was; I was a total random to him, and he'd literally never heard of me before. But he said that within two clicks on Google he understood what I did and what I was about, and so he said yes. The reason this worked is because I've worked hard on my brand consistency—and my Google results show it. Consistency is really important. It's not about having millions of followers; it's about being clear on what you're trying to achieve and what you have already achieved. It is crucial that your content that is publicly displayed reflects your intentions and who you are.

Nine Ways to Build a Solid Online Presence to Attract More Connections

Building a good reputation in your working life is important, and now that most of our lives are spent online, it matters what people see when they type our name into Google. Of course, we all make small mistakes or post something we wish we hadn't, but it's important to try to be mindful of what you put out online. Curating our online spaces is crucial to feeling in control of how you are presented to the outside world. Here are some lessons I've learned along the way:

1. AVOID RASH, ARGUMENTATIVE TWEETS

Have your digital footprint in mind whenever you feel drawn into an online argument. It's fine to have an opinion (of course!) but just ask yourself quickly: Do I want this to be accessible online forever? Will it look bad if I have to delete these comments? Even if you delete, it's still available somewhere. Plus, people like to screengrab things. We live in a fast-paced time of communication; it never hurts to pause for a moment and ask yourself whether you really need respond or whether it might look and feel better if you step away and take a pause. I find that sometimes when I get annoyed by something I see, it's helpful to write down my thoughts in a journal. I feel better because I have gotten my thoughts down on paper (where they might inform a piece of content I make at a later date) and I haven't gotten into a spiral of argumentative tweets for no reason. Arguing online often doesn't solve anything and only makes you feel worse.

2. CHECK BEFORE YOU POST (DUCKING AUTOCORRECT!)

Again, this fast-paced era of communication means we can fire things off left, right, and center. I'm a fan of tools like Grammarly, which help you craft emails with correct grammar and proofread for you. We've all had autocorrect nightmares, and they aren't the end of the world, but some things are really crucial to get right. Errors can instantly put someone off. It still matters to check things and for your content to be presentable even though we live in an emoji era.

3. CREATE YOUR OWN CATALOG OF CONTENT

One platform that works really well for someone else might not be the right one for you. You can't force it, and it's worth taking the time to figure out which platform helps you best express yourself.

>> Do you like making short videos? – Instagram.
>> Do you prefer short sentences? – Twitter.
>> Are you better at curating others' content? – Pinterest.
>> Do you want your presence to be minimal and powerful? – Create a static website (some websites are just a great simple design with a basic contact page, which can be very intriguing).

Pick a platform that shows your work off to its greatest advantage; don't sit across eight different social-media apps for the sake of it. It'll be a waste of your time and could dilute your message.

4. SELF-PROMOTE, BUT HAVE A BALANCE

The goal of self-promotion is to get more work. Always have this in mind. You are sharing your work for a reason, not just for the sake of it. Treat self-promotion as a strategy with a desired outcome. This will alleviate any moments of *Is this showing off?* If you have a purpose to sharing something (that you're proud of it, want people to employ you off the back of it, or show that you've collaborated with someone who aligns with your views), it will always feel intentional and genuine.

5. INVEST IN YOUR VISUALS

Visuals are really important, and if online searches might lead people to your page, they will make a decision on whether to work with you based on what they read and see. Words matter too, of course, but so do striking visuals. Invest in your design, color palette, headshots, and website usability. Visual branding should be a top priority. You could be the best at your job, but with an old website that doesn't work, you could easily put people off at the first click. I always invest in visuals because I know I will make that money back in more work booked.

6. HAVE A NEUTRAL EMAIL ADDRESS

It can be strangely off-putting when you meet someone and look down at their business card and their email address is FluffyChicken69@hotmail.com. Ideally, you should set up your own domain name.

7. CHECK THAT YOUR PERSONAL PAGES ARE ON PRIVATE

It's becoming the norm to have both public pages and private pages so that you are more in control of what can be publicly seen by all versus what you share with your friends and family (this is a good tactic for everyone, not just celebrities with private Instagram accounts). Your public business page can have a clear direction, and you can add personal touches to it as and when you want; your private pages can be freer. Even when you achieve your ideal work-life blend, it can be nice to have a space on the Internet that is just for you.

8. BUILD UP A GOOD FIRST PAGE OF GOOGLE RESULTS

Did you know that by opening a new incognito window on Google Chrome (for example) you can see what your search results on Google would show without your past Internet history skewing the results? You can monitor how it looks, what sort of things are pulled in from your social channels, etc.—it's good to be aware of how you display to others. Securing outside coverage about your business is a good strategy for improving your search results. If your name or business gets mentioned in mainstream online magazines, it'll most likely show in the first-page search results. After all, 75 percent of people will never scroll past the first page on a Google search.

Making sure you have a solid personal website presence is crucial too, by using keywords, consistency, and good design. But knowing what you want to achieve, and the purpose of your brand, is the first step. No amount of good design is going to help if you don't have a message. Be aware of what photos you upload, as your Google Images matter too when people search for you. (This section has reminded me of the creepy online tool called Awesome Baby Name that allows new parents to choose a name for their child based on website domain availability and SEO. Shudder.)

9. WRITE DOWN WHAT CATCHES YOUR EYE ONLINE

Inspiration on how to fine-tune my online presence in a business sense normally comes from noting what impresses me as a consumer or viewer. I make note of what stands out on my newsfeed: If something simple catches my eye, or I like the color of a logo, or a new website widget, or a short video. I'm not saying I straight up copy anything, but I actively notice what is working for me as a recipient of the content. Most companies engage in some sort of competitor research, and so should you.

Chapter 10

OUR RELATIONSHIP WITH MONEY

"Work is not your family. The only way work shows how much they care about you is by how much they pay you."

—AMINATOU SOW, the Cut, 2019

On Gaby Dunn's podcast *Bad with Money,* she asks her guests two questions:

1. What is your favorite sex position?
2. How much money is in your bank account?

Guests answer the first question awkwardly (but usually quite openly), but the second question is met with silence. Which one would you rather answer? Arguably, I would feel more exposed answering the second one.

I am a recovering bad-with-money person. Sometimes I drift back to my old ways if I'm having a stressful or emotional month, but the Internet has helped me a lot in overcoming my bad choices and spotting recurring habits. I read websites like the Financial Diet, which gives you true stories and practical advice too. I only recently discovered "financial health" and what it is to be "financially literate." Money is a language, and it's also something you need to practice getting good at. I love how blogging and the open nature of social media have made us more likely to discuss our mental and physical health, and I think the last taboo is talking openly about our financial health too.

A bad relationship with money can affect us in different ways: It can create strain on a relationship, can keep us up at night, make us unwell, can affect our motivation and sense of security. Having no money can cause stress due to worry, and suddenly making lots of it can also cause complications too. Being open about your financial health doesn't necessarily mean going around telling everyone your salary (though sharing salary and rate information with colleagues and your network is an important—though uncomfortable—way to ensure more fairness in the workplace). Money is intensely personal. But being more open can help us learn from each other. Making an effort to talk more about money can help us face our fears and tackle specific financial problems.

I couldn't write a book about being a multi-hyphenate without touching on money. It's an extremely important element to all of this, and being on top of your finances when you have multiple projects on the go is crucial. Of course, you can strategize and aim for a regular monthly income via your hyphens, but it will obviously be different from a static monthly salary from a single source. When you start to work for yourself, you have to keep track of and stay on top of multiple revenue streams.

I wish I'd learned more about money in school. Taxes, budgeting, retirement savings—these are all things that I had to figure out the hard way. I thought my student loan was free money, and I wasted it on stupid things. I had an overdraft that I combatted every month. I remember one year I took an ill-advised trip to Amsterdam on credit. My mum called me to say I'd been getting letters from my bank, warning me that I was racking up fees by going into overdraft so frequently. I broke down in tears—why was I so irresponsible? Why had I booked a vacation when I knew I couldn't afford it? It's like when you're on a "diet" and you end up eating more to sabotage yourself. I would try to save and feel deprived, so I ended up spending to feel better, which would lead me down a guilt spiral. I would find myself in vicious circles of doom. It is embarrassing to be in any sort of debt. It feels like a horrible secret. It was when other people began to be honest with me about their own debt that the weight started to lift and I managed to make changes, knowing I wasn't alone. It's hard to talk or think about money without there being an emotional reaction. It can bring up vulnerable memories, our worst fears, and comparison triggers. But everything is easier when you have people to talk to.

Having Backup

When it comes to work, we pull late nights, work weekends, and go over and above to impress and improve in pursuit of feeling special and needed by a company in return. We want to feel valuable. Companies sometimes call their employees partners or refer to themselves as a family as a way to make workers feel emotionally invested, when in fact a company is a business and every employee would be expendable if it were necessary. When it really comes down to it, human emotions aren't a priority when it comes to business decisions—the business always comes first.

The world we're in right now is more volatile every day. Having a side hustle or side skill isn't just a fun idea; it's becoming a way to stay on your feet. Once upon a time companies might house you, relocate you, help pay for your kids to go to school, and genuinely take care of you as a worker to make sure working at that company for life was desirable. Now it's different. When big changes happen—and none of us can foresee them until they are coming toward us—overhead costs like headcount are often the easiest to cut. Many workplaces are not future-proofing enough, and they are overly reactive instead of proactive. Do your job and do it well, but know that job security is far more precarious than it used to be. Workers are as dedicated as we always were, yet mergers and market contractions and layoffs continue at a record pace. This is why it is important to have more than one stream of income. If anything were to happen to your job or company, you have something to fall back on.

Making sure you have some sort of cushion is becoming more and more crucial, especially if you are a multi-hyphenate and don't have a traditional savings plan. One month can look different from the next. One month might be a super-duper moneymaking month, with many different projects all paying you at the same time or some big opportunities for sales or commissions coming in at once. And you might have months that are less fruitful, so it really matters how you manage your money.

THREE MONEY MANAGEMENT TIPS FOR WHEN YOU'RE SELF-EMPLOYED

1. Always make sure you are putting away a chunk of income for taxes (into a business savings account). After paying taxes, you can put the leftover amount into a personal savings account (I actually put half aside of all earnings into a separate account, to be extra safe!).
2. Work out which business expenses are deductible.
3. Look into getting an accountant—it saves so much stress!

Why Are We So Scared to Talk About Money?

Seven in ten people consider it rude or inappropriate to discuss personal money matters in a social setting, according to a survey by Ally Bank.[1] At a work event recently, someone came up to me and asked me very directly how much money I make. It wasn't the question that took me aback; it was how direct the question was. I don't think anyone had ever asked me so openly before. I ended up giving quite a broad answer that didn't reveal the specifics. I was vague about how it changes from month to month, which is true. The conversation forced me to reflect on why I found the whole subject awkward. Surely, if I want more honesty around money, I shouldn't have found it intrusive. Why is it that we find it difficult to talk specific numbers? I asked my community on Twitter how they would feel if it happened to them and asked them how much they earn. I received a mix of over two hundred responses.

Sophie Heawood, a journalist, replied: "Personally I find it completely mortifying. Anthropologically it varies massively between cultures but in the one I'm from it's rude." Music critic Miranda Sawyer replied: "I think it depends on who's asking. If it's a younger journalist, I'm happy to be open about how much I earn and what I do/say to get paid." Heawood then also agreed: "Oh if it was someone aspiring who needed to know specific rates and how to charge them I would def say. Not a random asking overall income." And then Miranda hit on why the subject is so difficult to discuss: "Money is so weird when you live in a capitalist society, totally wrapped up with personal/emotional/social worth instead of just financial." We want to be open to helping others, but money is wrapped up in so much emotion—about class, identity, literal worth—that it can make us feel vulnerable.

The United Kingdom's top YouTuber, Zoella, wrote: "[It] depends who is asking and why they are asking. If I felt a friend in the industry was being swizzled, I'd say what they should be getting, based on what I know from my own earnings etc. But generally, there's never a need to talk about it and a lot of it is just nosiness!"

Karina Brisby said: "Aussie culture is more open to salaries conversations, learnt that very quickly when I moved to UK." Writer Kieran Yates said: "Can't speak for everyone but largely in South Asian communities being asked how much you earn is just par for the course."

Becca DP said: "I have actively been told in the past 'do not tell anyone else on the team what your salary is' which felt very grubby." This has also happened to me. I negotiated a really good salary in a job once and then was told not to tell the others, as it would make the other members of the team resent me.

Luiza Sauma said: "The idea of it being 'rude' has been drilled into us by ppl who want to hide their wealth. Secrecy around salaries leads to wage disparity."

The responses were, obviously, mixed. Some people were horrified; some raised the point that transparency helps people not get taken advantage of. A female friend of mine accidentally found out what money her (also female, same level) colleague made, and the difference between their salaries was huge. She was distraught. It's extremely upsetting to learn about pay disparities, but they are more likely to continue when salaries are shrouded in secrecy. Even though I can hand-on-heart say that I don't think money should be synonymous with "success" (there are definitely times I've felt successful in my work with peanuts in my bank account), there is no denying that making money for something you've worked hard on feels really good. Sending an invoice for a big sum feels fantastic! Money gives us freedom. It validates our work. On the one hand, we feel like money doesn't equal success, and on the other hand, we feel it is an indicator of being taken seriously.

Talking about making money is tricky and does depend on the tone. An Instagram photographer and online consultant recently announced that she made £200,000 in one year from her Internet job, sitting at her kitchen table in the middle of the countryside. She runs e-courses online and consults on digital growth. Despite the high figure, her announcement didn't come across as show-off or crass; instead, her tone made it feel inspiring to know that someone can work for themselves in a niche and thriving industry and make a living. It was said to prove a point—these new roles that are often judged as not being "real" jobs can actually earn you a very good salary indeed.

Being Open About Money Helps When Asking for More Money

Having a community you can turn to is important when you have a multi-hyphenate career and you need to compare and contrast rates and ask for advice. You can quickly check whether your ballpark figure sounds about right or what sort of rates other people have commanded and why. It also means that if you can't take on a piece of work, you can offer it out to someone in your network, and they'll, in turn, send work your way in the future. You end up getting a lot back when you share with others instead of being secretive and keeping things to yourself.

It gives you an added boost of confidence when asking for more money, too. You feel more confident when you have a grasp of the market rate. Cindy Gallop once gave advice to women who might be unsure how much to ask for if they are self-employed or taking on a new job, and I always think of it. She said this: "You should ask for the highest number you can utter without actually bursting out laughing."[2] Seeing as most people try to bring down your fee anyway, you might as well go in high.

THREE TIPS ON NEGOTIATING A FEE

1. Get the client to offer a fee first, before giving your rate, as their budget might be higher than your set rate.
2. Ask for more—see whether there is wiggle room (always worth asking!) and see what added extras you can offer to your service.
3. Don't accept anything too low with the promise of a higher fee next time. There might not be a next project for a long time, and you will lose out.

Top tip: If the company or client pays you late, you are allowed to ask for late fees. In many places (like the United Kingdom and New York City), this is protected by law. Look into your local laws and regulations for more info.

Making Money Unconventionally

According to business writer Manoj Arora, most millionaires have seven income streams.[3] I knew that my fear of being made redundant (after seeing it happen to countless friends) would ultimately mean I would have to set up income streams that I could potentially control. I could see trends in what some of my friends were doing—monetizing blogs, websites or marketplaces, podcasts, and their digital services. I knew that instead of sitting in one location, working for one company, I could spread myself across multiple projects and have those different streams of income that I've always dreamed about. I could often earn money from one to four different projects in one week, potentially quadrupling my income. It also suited my personality. I am a fast worker, and I get impatient and bored easily. I respond really well to juggling multiple projects. I love putting my heart and soul and best self into a project, and then I also enjoy wrapping up and moving on to something else I'm passionate about. In my office job I learned how to juggle multiple tasks as part of one role—it was my bootcamp. So, I wondered, what if I could use my time more wisely, without needing to waste my time commuting or having endless meetings?

A great resource to see how other people manage their side hustles is the Starling Bank blog. They interview different side hustlers about how they balance their gigs alongside their day jobs and what their biggest money-management challenge is. Morena Fiore-Kirby, owner of Kodes Accessories, wrote, "It's easy to get carried away investing in new materials and experiments. I always have ideas bouncing around in my head as a crafter, and being my own boss means I can approve any purchase. It's a challenge to keep my feet on the ground and concentrate on what's necessary and viable."[4] Managing your own costs and keeping track of everything are common challenges for multi-hyphenates. When it comes to tracking, that's where some online tools and apps can come in handy. Examples include Unsplurge, which is an iOS budget app that helps you save, and Clarity Money, an app that helps you track the granular details of your spending and reminds you to cancel any of those wasteful subscriptions you forgot about, for example.

Building your own ecosystem of income streams that you can keep up with can pay off. There are so many ways to make money online. You might teach an e-course, pick up a consulting project, or sell a product via an online marketplace. One example from my life came about when I told a friend that a lot of people were buying books from my recommendations online. She said I should set up an Amazon Associates account. Now I get a small percentage of every sale when someone buys a book from a link I shared. This is one example of many, but we can monetize more than we think.

SEVEN WAYS TO MONETIZE A SIDE HUSTLE

1. Sell your product (whatever it might be) via an ecommerce site like Shopify.
2. Pitch yourself to a single big sponsor for the year—essentially seek an investment from one company for a long-term partnership, as opposed to lots of mini collaborations.
3. Podcasts can be monetized through platforms like Libsyn, Acast, and Podbean.
4. Build a newsletter and subscriber base, and use them to partner with other companies.
5. Sell an e-book or webinar online.
6. Use affiliated links on social media (for example, Amazon Associates), where a purchase made through one of your links earns you a percentage of the sale.
7. Crowdfund a side hustle via companies like Kickstarter, Indiegogo, or Unbound (if it is a book).

Our Money Goals Are Personal and All Different

The *Cut's* "Money Mom" advice column is dedicated to helping people with their money. *Refinery29*'s incredibly popular "Money

Diaries" feature documents the spending of people in many different kinds of financial circumstances. This kind of content is catnip to readers because the stories offer windows into lives very different from our own. Someone wrote the Money Mom asking whether they will ever have enough money. The Money Mom replied, "What does 'enough' money mean to you, really? It's subjective, of course, but for most people it involves a measure of independence."[5] This rang so true. In my own life, I've found that what is "enough" to my friends is often strikingly different from what is "enough" for me. The question made me ask myself: *How much do I want? What is my personal level of enough?* My answer is going to be different from yours, as yours will be different from mine, your friends', and even your family's. "Enough" is personal, and we should dig deep and examine how much we truly want.

Working out how much is "enough" in practical terms means first figuring out how much you need in order to live each month. Calculating this figure allows us to make future plans more easily. Knowing exactly how much you need to cover your expenses means you know how much more you need if, for example, you wanted to take a month off to travel or invest in a new side hustle. It is empowering to be on top of your finances. Knowing the base amount you need to live on and seeing how much you could save by earning beyond that give you a sense of control and independence.

That's not to say we should squash ourselves down and think that our "enough" should be just enough to live on, or less than we deserve. I spoke about this with Anne Boden, the CEO of the mobile app Starling Bank. In a previous job, when Anne asked for a raise, her boss replied: "But your salary is enough for you." What does "enough for you" mean? Was it enough because she's a woman? Because of her class background? Because of where she grew up? Because of her age? Our marker of "enough" should be totally up to us. Knowing what enough money looks like to us doesn't mean settling for someone else's definition; it means being confident in our own personal goals.

HOW MUCH DOES MONEY MATTER TO YOU?
- » Is a high salary your main motivator?
- » What material things make you happiest?
- » What nonmaterial things make you happy?
- » How quickly does the buzz of a new purchase wear off?
- » How much do you *need* every month to live?
- » How much do you need every month *to live the life you want to live?*

Make Yourself a Very Simple Budget Tracker

Before I dived fully into the Multi-Hyphen Life, I calculated exactly what I needed each month and hashed out my exit plan accordingly. I was able to track and stash away any small leftovers each month (knowing I was going to quit and would need a cushion), and I figured out a solid number of what I would need to make each month if I fully worked for myself. My system was roughly this:

- » Calculate total income from all different projects.
- » Write a list of all repeat expenses every single month.
- » Put expenses into categories (utilities, transportation, insurance, debt repayment, miscellaneous, etc.) and total them.
- » Calculate the balance: total income minus total expenses. This is what you need every month.
- » In the event that you may have anything left over, stash it away into savings.

It can feel like a sacrifice at the beginning. The benefits are huge once you set up your multiple income streams, but this adjustment period can feel like you're going backward for a time. It's worth it in the end to establish your new path, one that is freer, more creative.

Creating Your Own Cushion

The word "pension" always felt quite alien to me. I moved jobs so many times that I kept rolling any workplace retirement savings over, losing track of what I'd put in and what was matched or not matched by the company. It was a good perk, but I knew I would reap the full benefits only if I stayed at one company for a long, long time. I read a tip that said you should aim to save $1,000 for retirement every month. Talk about unrelatable and sort of impossible! Who can easily save that much? I decided to think in terms of a "cushion" instead of a "pension" and started working toward making a cushion for my future.

Millennials have a different relationship with money from their parents as a result of coming into the workforce during a recession and housing crisis. Unlike our parents, two-thirds of millennials have student loans and credit card debt. Far fewer of us own property. We are so in debt that our relationship with money has been tainted from the get-go. But despite our different circumstances, we still need to think about retirement, and the earlier we are aware of its importance, the better. There will be a time, for all of us, when we want (or need) to stop working.

According to an article in the *Financial Times*, "only 16 percent of respondents said they know how much to save to achieve the hoped-for standard of living in retirement."[6] According to the National Institute on Retirement Security, 66 percent of working millennials in the United States have no retirement savings at all. It's clear that the standard retirement savings system isn't working for many. If more people are turning to multi-hyphenate lifestyles, we need to figure out a new way to start saving and stashing away for the future. Working a cushion into your plans now will pay off later.

Stop Comparing Your Bank Account

In vulnerable moments, I can momentarily get down in the dumps feeling jealous about how much money someone else seems to have (usually based on something as woolly as their Instagram feed).

Even though money is not number one on my list of what makes me feel successful, I can't help but make occasional judgments and assumptions about how much people around me earn. But the truth is we don't know how much people are earning or what's in someone's bank account. Katherine Ormerod, a writer who has a website called Work Work Work, wrote a piece titled "Money's Too Tight to Mention" where she admitted that there was often a gulf between what she was showing on Instagram and what was in her actual bank account: "Not everything in my life or on Instagram is a free-dinner, but a lot of it is. This so exponentially misrepresents the true picture of my financial situation."

I have interviewed both high-profile celebrities and "Internet famous" people with huge online followings who have hardly any money and people with low-paying jobs who have mastered the art of saving. I think a lot of the mystery and taboo around money conversations are because employers don't benefit from wage transparency. We know that openness about pay—and pay disparities—leads to tough conversations about workplace equity. It costs companies money to pay everyone fairly.

In an ideal world we would be fully transparent when it comes to money because there should be nothing to hide. As a multi-hyphenate, it is easier to be more transparent about money because you can talk about fees on a project-by-project basis, rather than revealing your one salary. I find it easy to talk about my fees with fellow multi-hyphenates, and I know my worth down to the hour. We compare and contrast and discuss rates. I've felt much more empowered charging for my time because I'm confident in my market rate. My salary used to feel like something I should keep secret. With the way I work now, I feel empowered, in control, and freer to talk more openly about money.

THE END (SORT OF)

Congrats, you made it to the final chapter! I hope that you feel pumped up and ready to spread your multi-hyphenate wings and that you now have a list of notes and ideas about how to expand your working portfolio. This is the part in most business or career books where the author gives you a tidy little wrap-up, a motivational ending where all loose ends are tied up before you close the book and carry on with your life. Maybe it would include some big predictions too, telling you that if you follow the plan, success is virtually guaranteed. But the whole point of this book is that there is no comprehensive plan that will address all possible future scenarios. The working world is changing, and we are in the change right now. We don't know exactly where the workplace is going or what our individual futures hold. But what we can do is empower ourselves in the meantime. We can use the tools in our pockets to maintain relevancy, carry on future-proofing ourselves, and keep in mind the fact that a lot of jobs are yet to be invented. We can let ourselves get overwhelmed, or we can be energized by the potential opportunities. We get to reinvent ourselves, learn new skills, collaborate, and find new, not-so-obvious ways to use technology to make our lives easier and our work more interesting. We can work in a way that frees up more of our time and makes use of all our multifaceted human selves. We get to break out of the boxes. We get to quit and start again.

My goal with this book is to help you unpick the entrenched beliefs about work we grew up absorbing and holding as gospel. This book is a guide to thinking about things differently. It is not about waking up tomorrow and handing in your resignation letter; it is about taking small, consistent risks and opening yourself up to opportunities. It's about stepping outside of one defined career box. If you have been thinking about making any changes to your working life, now is a good time. It's important to invest in yourself. While big restructures and industry shifts continue around you, you can start your side project, launch that website, sell your services independently, and experiment with what you find. Now's the time for us to take matters into our own hands. It really is time to rip up the rule book and chart our own courses—which aren't as scary as they sound. It is scarier to plod along as if nothing has changed while the rug edges out from under our feet.

Branch out and conquer that thing you've wanted to do. Do it in your spare or stolen time or all of your time. I am rooting for you.

It Might Feel Like a Sacrifice at the Beginning

It is normal for something to feel like a bit of a step backward before you go forward. Self-doubt, I've learned, can actually be a pretty useful emotion. It niggles at you and forces you to analyze your current situation and think about whether there is anything you need to change or do. *The Power of Negative Emotion* by Todd Kashdan and Robert Biswas-Diener posits that certain difficult emotions can guide you. Feeling jealous? It might be a sign that you want to go after something. Feeling full of fear and self-doubt? It might be because you've decided to take the plunge. Feeling angry? It might be because it's within reach but you haven't found the tools yet to really bring your idea to fruition. Behind each of these negative feelings is a sign that you're on your way to your goal. Embrace these icky emotions and use them to spur you on. You just have to pick off a few layers of the onion to work out how you really feel. Sometimes, things feel rocky, but it doesn't mean you've made a bad decision. When I left my full-time job after years of side hustling, I felt the most vulnerable I've ever felt, but the benefits after months of self-doubt were so worth it in the end. Things take time to bloom.

Embrace Your Own Unique Magic Powers

One of the joys of a Multi-Hyphen Life is that you are at the center of your career and you can bring your (wide-ranging!) unique skills to the table. Are you good with people? Are you fiercely independent? Are you very adaptable and can work from anywhere? Can you learn new things quickly? Are you good at coming up with out-of-the-box ideas? Listen to how people compliment you. We all have things we are good at, even if they're not the usual extroverted skills rewarded in a big corporate workplace. Keep an eye on the quieter things that will give you an edge over your competition. Remember these skills, nurture them, and know there is a place for them in your multi-hyphened career path.

Reclaim Your Time

As Congresswoman Maxine Waters so famously said: "I'm reclaiming my time!" Reclaiming your time is a key benefit to the Multi-Hyphen Life. Time feels like one of the biggest luxuries, but we shouldn't treat flexible working opportunities like a privilege for only a small number of people. They should be more widely available to everyone. Having time to ourselves—in even the smallest amounts— helps us grow, learn, and be our best selves. Now's the time to ask for some flexibility at work, even if it's only a couple of hours a week, and, if you're in a position to, to advocate for more flexibility for everyone across the board. We also need to make an effort to disconnect from our online worlds more often. Reclaim your time from mindless scrolling.

Permission Granted

Workplace hierarchies are changing, what we want from work is changing, and we don't get a "permission slip" from the same places anymore. Every time I lead a work-related event or workshop, 99 percent of the people who come up to me don't ask me for advice; they ask me for permission. They tell me their business plans in detail, they tell me all about the preparation they've already done, the ideas in their head, the steps they want to take, the passion behind it, and all they seem to want is reassurance. It's made me realize just how much we stand in our own way by simply not giving ourselves the permission to go for it. Give yourself the permission to give it—whatever it is—a try.

Be Open to Change

Change is good. Change can be scary, but it can also be wonderful. Freelance talent collective Akin recently published a study on "changemakers." Changemakers don't belong to one generation or location, but rather they are "a group of people defined by their values and attitudes"—they're progressive, they influence, and they drive change. Multi-hyphenates—those who are looking for a different kind of lifestyle, who are open to new ways of doing things—are changemakers. It is estimated there are 455 million of us globally, according to Nielsen. You—reading this—you are a changemaker, because otherwise you wouldn't have picked up this book. You are not alone in your quest for a different working life. There are millions of people around us who are looking to make these same changes. When we empower ourselves at work, we empower ourselves in life. Let's not be afraid to be many different things.

NOTES

INTRODUCTION

1. Brian Rashid, "The Rise of the Freelancer Economy," *Forbes* (Jan. 26, 2016), https://www.forbes.com/sites/brianrashid/2016/01/26/the-rise-of-the-freelancer-economy/#1dd084ea3bdf

2. Daniel B. Kline, "Does Technology Make Us More Productive Workers?" *Boston.com* (Feb. 22, 2013), https://www.boston.com/news/business/2013/02/22/does-technology-make-us-more-productive-workers

3. Anna Robaton, "Why So Many Americans Hate Their Jobs," CBS News (March 31, 2017), https://www.cbsnews.com/news/why-so-many-americans-hate-their-jobs/

4. Chris Stokel-Walker, "People Start Hating Their Jobs at Age 35," Bloomberg (Aug. 22, 2017), https://www.bloomberg.com/news/articles/2017-08-21/people-start-hating-their-jobs-at-age-35

CHAPTER 1

1. *Oxford Living Dictionary* (accessed December 2017), https://en.oxforddictionaries.com/definition/success

2. Kara Melchers, "Why Choose the Career Ladder When There's a Climbing Frame?" *It's Nice That* (Nov. 7, 2017), https://www.itsnicethat.com/articles/creative-passion-projects-becoming-your-full-time-job-opinion-071117

3. Gemma Askham, "Forget the Career Ladder—Here's How to Get Ahead at Work (without Being a #girlboss)" *Glamour* (Sept. 4, 2017), http://www.glamourmagazine.co.uk/article/how-to-get-ahead-at-work

4. Vicki Salemi, "76% of American Workers Say They Get the 'Sunday Night Blues,'" Monster (accessed December 2017), https://www.monster.com/career-advice/article/its-time-to-eliminate-sunday-night-blues-0602

5. Ginny Marvin, "U.S. Podcast Audiences Keep Growing, 62 Million Listening Weekly," *Marketing Land* (March 7, 2019), https://marketingland.com/u-s-podcast-audiences-keep-growing-62-million-listening-weekly-258179

6. Elaine Welteroth, "When I Moved to New York City …" Instagram (Jan. 14, 2018), https://www.instagram.com/p/Bd76UOXFo1T/?hl=en&taken-by=elainewelteroth

7. Neville Hobson, "Why the Gig Economy Fits Well with the Lives of Baby Boomers," *Neville Hobson* (June 26, 2017), https://www.nevillehobson.com/2017/06/26/gig-economy-baby-boomers/

8. Jennifer Calfas, "Millennials Want Jobs and Education, Not Marriage and Kids," *Time* (April 20, 2017), http://time.com/4748357/milennials-values-census-report/

9. Nikki Graf, Anna Brown, and Eileen Patten, "The Narrowing, but Persistent, Gender Gap in Pay," Pew Research Center (March 22, 2019), https://www.pewresearch.org/fact-tank/2019/03/22/gender-pay-gap-facts/

10. Haley Nahman, "The Elusive Definition of 'Success' (and Why It Makes Us Feel Bad)" Man Repeller (April 4, 2019), https://www.manrepeller.com/2019/04/what-is-success.html

11. Vicky Spratt, "Ask an Adult: Why Can't I Concentrate in an Open Plan Office?" *Grazia* (April 12, 2016), https://graziadaily.co.uk/life/real-life/ask-adult-cant-concentrate-open-plan-office/

12. William Belk, "58% of High-Performance Employees Say They Need More Quiet Work Spaces," CNBC (last updated March 16, 2017), https://www.cnbc.com/2017/03/15/58-of-high-performance-employees-say-they-need-more-quiet-work-spaces.html

13. Paul Robertson, "Open Plan Offices Are a Health and Productivity Risk—Canada Life," *Cover* (May 14, 2014), https://www.covermagazine.co.uk/cover/news/2344756/open-plan-offices-are-a-health-and-productivity-risk-canada-life%20

14. Justin McCurry, "Clocking Off: Japan Calls Time on Long-Hours Work Culture," *The Guardian* (Feb. 22, 2015), https://www.theguardian.com/world/2015/feb/22/japan-long-hours-work-culture-overwork-paid-holiday-law

15. Steve Chao and Liz Gooch, "The Country with the World's Worst Drink Problem," Al Jazeera (Feb. 7, 2016), http://www.aljazeera.com/indepth/features/2016/02/country-world-worst-drink-problem-160202120308308.html

16. Natalie Sisson, "[245] The Traditional Workplace Is Coming to an End" [podcast], *The Suitcase Entrepreneur* (March 11, 2016), https://suitcaseentrepreneur.com/traditional-workplace-coming-end/

CHAPTER 2

1. John Mauldin, "Generational Chaos Ahead," Mauldin Economics (June 19, 2016), https://www.mauldineconomics.com/frontlinethoughts/generational-chaos-ahead

2. American Management Association, "Leading the Four Generations at Work" (accessed April 18, 2018), http://www.amanet.org/training/articles/leading-the-four-generations-at-work.aspx

3. "Generation Z," Wikipedia (last edited Feb. 28, 2018), https://en.wikipedia.org/wiki/Generation_Z

4. Pip Wilson, "Why Technology Is Key to Workplace Diversity," *HuffPost* (last updated March 3, 2018), http://www.huffingtonpost.co.uk/pip-wilson/whytechnology-is-key-to-_b_15080720.html

5. "George Orwell," Wikiquote (accessed April 8, 2018), https://en.wikiquote.org/wiki/George_Orwell

6. William Cummings, "The Malignant Myth of the Millennial," *USA Today* (May 11, 2017), https://www.usatoday.com/story/news/nation/2017/05/11/millennial-myth/100982920/

7. Jared Lindzon, "The Problem with Generational Stereotypes at Work," *Fast Company* (March 23, 2016), https://www.fastcompany.com/3057905/the-problem-with-generational-stereotypes-at-work

8. Rt Hon Esther McVey MP, "Employers Need to Wake Up to Urgent Labour Market Challenges," *theHRDIRECTOR* (Oct. 23, 2017), https://www.thehrdirector.com/business-news/employment/employers-labour-market-challenges/

9. Beth Snyder Bulik, "Boomers—Yes, Boomers—Spend the Most on Tech," *Ad Age* (Oct. 11, 2010), http://adage.com/article/digital/consumer-electronics-baby-boomers-spend-tech/146391/

10. Patrick Foster, "One in Four Over-65s Use Social Media, after Massive Rise in 'Instagrans,'" *The Telegraph* (Aug. 4, 2016), http://www.telegraph.co.uk/news/2016/08/04/one-in-four-over-65s-use-social-media-after-massive-rise-in-inst/

11. Hannah Furness, "Rise of the 'Social Seniors' as Number of Over-75s on Facebook Doubles," *The Telegraph* (June 14, 2017), http://www.telegraph.co.uk/news/2017/06/14/rise-social-seniors-number-over-75s-facebook-doubles/

12. Georgina Fuller, "The Generation of Slashie Employees," AAT Comment (Feb. 20, 2017), http://www.aatcomment.org.uk/the-generation-of-slashie-employees/

13. Jean M. Twenge, "Have Smartphones Destroyed a Generation?" *The Atlantic* (Aug. 3, 2017), https://www.theatlantic.com/amp/article/534198/

14. "2017 Edelman Trust Barometer," Edelman, https://www.edelman.com/research/2017-edelman-trust-barometer

15. Yuval Noah Harari, "The Meaning of Life in a World without Work," *The Guardian* (May 8, 2017), https://www.theguardian.com/technology/2017/may/08/virtual-reality-religion-robots-sapiens-book

16. Michael Smolensky and Lynne Lamberg, *The Body Clock Guide to Better Health*, NASW, https://www.nasw.org/users/llamberg/larkowl.htm

17. Jonathan Chew, "Why Millennials Would Take a $7,600 Pay Cut for a New Job," *Fortune* (April 8, 2016), http://fortune.com/2016/04/08/fidelity-millennial-study-career/

18. Rebecca Greenfield, "The Office Hierarchy Is Officially Dead," *Sydney Morning Herald* (March 4, 2016), http://www.smh.com.au/business/workplace-relations/the-office-hierarchy-is-officially-dead-20160303-gna5o6.html

19. Aaron Dignan, "The Org Chart Is Dead," *The Ready* (Feb. 27, 2016), https://medium.com/the-ready/the-org-chart-is-dead-e1d76eca9ce0

20. Zainab Mudallal, "Airbnb Will Soon Be Booking More Rooms Than the World's Largest Hotel Chains," *Quartz* (Jan. 20, 2015), https://qz.com/329735/airbnb-will-soon-be-booking-more-rooms-than-the-worlds-largest-hotel-chains/

21. Emily Ramshaw, "How Phillip Picardi Landed a Major Magazine Gig by the Age of 25," *Coveteur* (Aug. 18, 2018), http://coveteur.com/2016/08/18/deskside-phillip-picardi-teen-vogue-digital-editorial-director/

22. Ronald Alsop, "Why Bosses Won't 'Like' Generation Z," BBC (March 5, 2015), http://www.bbc.com/capital/story/20150304-the-attention-deficit-generation

23. Charlie Kim, "Maslow's Hierarchy of Needs: Updated," *HuffPost* (last updated Dec. 6, 2017), https://www.huffingtonpost.com/charlie-kim/maslows-hierarchy-of-need_b_4235665.html

24. The College Board, Trends in Student Aid 2013. Calculations based on average per-student borrowing in 1980 and 2010. Michael Hobbes, "FML: Why Millennials Are Facing the Scariest Financial Future of Any Generation Since the Great Depression," *Huffington Post Highline*, https://highline.huffingtonpost.com/articles/en/poor-millennials/?mobile=1

25. Kathleen Davis, "The Rise of Social Media as a Career (Infographic)," *Entrepreneur* (Oct. 1, 2013), https://www.entrepreneur.com/article/228651

26. Cathy Davidson, "65% of Future Jobs Haven't Been Invented Yet? Cathy Davidson Responds to Cathy Davidson and the BBC," HASTAC (May 31, 2017), https://www.hastac.org/blogs/cathy-davidson/2017/05/31/65-future-jobs-havent-been-invented-yet-cathy-davidson-responds

27. Kim Cassady, "3 Ways Technology Influences Generational Divides at Work," *Entrepreneur* (March 29, 2017), https://www.entrepreneur.com/article/290763

28. Randstad and Future Workplace, "Gen Z and Millennials Collide at Work" [report] (accessed December 2017), http://experts.randstadusa.com/hubfs/Randstad_GenZ_Millennials_Collide_Report.pdf

29. Alina Dizik, "The Next Generation of Jobs Won't Be Made Up of Professions," BBC (April 24, 2017)

30. Josh Bersin, "The Future of Work: It's Already Here—and Not as Scary as You Think," *Forbes* (Sept. 21, 2016), https://www.forbes.com/sites/joshbersin/2016/09/21/the-future-of-work-its-already-here-and-not-as-scary-as-you-think/#2d692e64bf53

CHAPTER 3

1. Freddie Harrel, "About Freddie Harrel" *Freddie Harrel* [blog] (accessed April 18, 2018)

2. Chase Jarvis, "The Future of Work Is Here: The Skill Economy," chasejarvis.com (Nov. 24, 2016), http://www.chasejarvis.com/blog/the-future-of-work-is-here-the-skill-economy/

3. Muhammad Yunus, quotation in Reid Hoffman and Ben Casnocha's *The Start-up of You*, London: Random House Business Books 2013, http://www.randomhouse.com/highschool/catalog/display.pperl?isbn=9780307888907&view=excerpt

4. Side Hustle Nation, "What Is a Side Hustle?' (May 13, 2013) https://www.sidehustlenation.com/what-is-a-side-hustle/

5. Kevin Roose, "Survey Says: 92 percent of Software Developers Are Men," Splinter (April 8, 2015), https://splinternews.com/survey-says-92-percent-of-software-developers-are-men-1793846921

6. "Caitlin Moran and Alex Kozloff" [video], IAB UK, (Nov. 14, 2016), https://www.youtube.com/watch?v=OxoRigaGaZI

7. Joshua Sophy, "More Than 1 in 4 Millennials Work a Side Hustle," *Small Business Trends* (July 20, 2017), https://smallbiztrends.com/2017/07/millennial-side-hustle-statistics.html

8. "Fifth of UK workers consider launching a 'side hustle' for extra cash or to pursue a passion," *Independent* (Oct. 4, 2017), https://www.independent.co.uk/news/business/news/side-hustle-uk-workers-extra-cash-passion-godaddy-startup-matthew-taylor-a7981896.html

9. Lydia Dishman, "How the Gig Economy Will Change In 2017," *Fast Company* (Jan. 5, 2017), https://www.fastcompany.com/3066905/how-the-gig-economy-will-change-in-2017

10. Jayne Robinson can be found on Twitter and Instagram under the handle @JayneKitsch

CHAPTER 4

1. "Audrey Gelman: Co-Founder of The Wing," Cuyana, https://www.cuyana.com/stories/essential-women-audrey-gelman.html

2. Mikel E. Belicove, "A New Study Reveals the Power of First Impressions Online," *Entrepreneur* (March 14, 2012), https://www.entrepreneur.com/article/223150

3. Clay Routledge, PhD, "On the Modern Self—an Interview with Will Storr," *Psychology Today* (Aug. 19, 2017)

4. Elizabeth Segran, "How Hiding Your True Self at Work Can Hurt Your Career," *Fast Company* (Sept. 17, 2015), https://www.fastcompany.com/3051111/how-hiding-your-true-self-at-work-can-hurt-your-career

5. Jennifer Miller, "Leadership Tips for the Modern Fluid Workforce," InPower Coaching (June 27, 2017), https://inpowercoaching.com/leadership-tips-modern-fluid-workforce/

6. Cathy Engelbert and John Hagel, "Radically Open: Tom Friedman on Jobs, Learning, and the Future of Work," *Deloitte Insights* (July 31, 2017), https://dupress.deloitte.com/dup-us-en/deloitte-review/issue-21/tom-friedman-interview-jobs-learning-future-of-work.html

7. Kenneth R. Rosen, "How to Recognize Burnout before You're Burned Out," *The New York Times* (Sept. 5, 2017), https://www.nytimes.com/2017/09/05/smarter-living/workplace-burnout-symptoms.html?sl_l=1&sl_rec=editorial&referer=

8. Jackee Holder, "How Creativity Boosts Your Mental Health and Wellbeing," Welldoing.org (Feb. 18, 2016), https://welldoing.org/article/how-creativity-boosts-your-mental-health-wellbeing

9. Lydia Ruffles, "Art and Soul: How Sparking Your Creativity Helps You Stay Well," *The Guardian* (Nov. 5, 2017), https://amp.theguardian.com/lifeandstyle/2017/nov/05/art-and-soul-how-sparking-creativity-helps-you-stay-well

CHAPTER 5

1. Lisa M. Gerry, "10 Signs You're Burning Out—and What to Do about It," *Forbes* (April 1, 2013)

2. Katie Forster, "Third of UK Workers Experiencing Anxiety, Depression or Stress, Survey Finds," *Independent* (July 6, 2017), http://www.independent.co.uk/news/health/uk-workers-depression-stress-anxiety-survey-a7827656.html

3. Kenneth R. Rosen, "How to Recognize Burnout before You're Burned Out," *The New York Times* (Sept. 5, 2017), https://www.nytimes.com/2017/09/05/smarter-living/workplace-burnout-symptoms.html

4. Jacquelyn Smith, "Here's Why Workplace Stress Is Costing Employers $300 Billion a Year," *Business Insider* (June 6, 2016), http://uk.businessinsider.com/how-stress-at-work-is-costing-employers-300-billion-a-year-2016-6?r=US&IR=T

5. Peter Fleming, "Do You Work More Than 39 Hours a Week? Your Job Could Be Killing You," *The Guardian* (Jan. 15, 2018), https://www.theguardian.com/lifeandstyle/2018/jan/15/is-28-hours-ideal-working-week-for-healthy-life

6. David Derbyshire, "Daytime Nap 'Is as Refreshing as a Night's Sleep,'" *The Telegraph* (June 23, 2003), http://www.telegraph.co.uk/news/worldnews/northamerica/usa/1433851/Daytime-nap-is-as-refreshing-as-a-nights-sleep.html

7. "Napping," National Sleep Foundation (accessed December 2017), https://sleepfoundation.org/sleep-topics/napping

8. The Daily Dozers, "8 Famous Nappers in History," MattressFirm (March 13, 2017), https://www.mattressfirm.com/blog/community-culture/8-famous-nappers-history/

9. Hilary Brueck, "'You Can Sleep When You're Dead' Is Actually Deadly Advice, According to Experts," *Business Insider* (Nov. 11, 2017), http://uk.businessinsider.com/how-much-sleep-is-enough-health-risks-dangers-of-sleep-deprivation-2017-11?utm_source=pocket&utm_medium=email&utm_campaign=pockethits&r=US&IR=T

10. Dan Schawbel, "Cali Williams Yost: Why We Have to Rethink Work Life Balance," *Forbes* (Jan. 9, 2013), https://www.forbes.com/sites/danschawbel/2013/01/08/cali-williams-yost-why-we-have-to-rethink-work-life-balance/#6512b65331d6

11. Max Chafkin, "Yahoo's Marissa Mayer on Selling a Company while Trying to Turn It Around," *Bloomberg Businessweek* (Aug. 4, 2016), https://www.bloomberg.com/features/2016-marissa-mayer-interview-issue/

12. Lev Grossman, "Runner-up: Tim Cook, the Technologist," *Time* (Dec. 19, 2012), http://poy.time.com/2012/12/19/runner-up-tim-cook-the-technologist/

13. Tony Poulos, "Should Untrained Under-18s Be Banned by Law from Social Media?" *DisruptiveViews* (Oct. 17, 2017), https://disruptiveviews.com/under-18s-banned-social-media/

14. Cathy Engelbert and John Hagel, "Radically Open: Tom Friedman on Jobs, Learning, and the Future of Work," *Deloitte Insights* (July 31, 2017), https://dupress.deloitte.com/dup-us-en/deloitte-review/issue-21/tom-friedman-interview-jobs-learning-future-of-work.html

15. Kim Janssen, "Social Media May Be as Bad as Smoking, Kickstarter CEO Tells Ashton Kutcher," *Chicago Tribune* (July 28, 2016), http://www.chicagotribune.com/news/chicagoinc/ct-ashton-kutcher-kickstarter-0729-chicago-inc-20160728-story.html

16. Lynn Enright, "Why Is Everything So Urgent? and What's It Doing to Our Brains?" *The Pool* (Nov. 17, 2017)

17. Roger McNamee, "How Facebook and Google Threaten Public Health—and Democracy," *The Guardian* (Nov. 11, 2017), https://amp.theguardian.com/commentisfree/2017/nov/11/facebook-google-public-health-democracy

18. Patrick Nelson, "We Touch Our Phones 2,617 Times a Day, Says Study," *Network World* (July 7, 2016), https://www.networkworld.com/article/3092446/smartphones/we-touch-our-phones-2617-times-a-day-says-study.html

19. Paul Lewis, "'Our Mind Can Be Hijacked': the Tech Insiders Who Fear a Smartphone Dystopia," *The Guardian* (Oct. 6, 2017), https://www.theguardian.com/technology/2017/oct/05/smartphone-addiction-silicon-valley-dystopia?CMP=share_btn_tw

20. Amy B. Wang (*Washington Post*), "Ex-Facebook Executive Says Social Media Are Destroying Society," *Houston Chronicle* (updated Dec. 13, 2017), http://www.chron.com/business/technology/article/Ex-Facebook-executive-says-social-media-is-12425734.php

21. Martha Lane Fox, "Technology Is a Marvel—Now Let's Make It Moral," *The Guardian* (April 10, 2017), https://www.theguardian.com/commentisfree/2017/apr/10/ethical-technology-women-britain-internet

22. Jess Commons, "How Did World News Drive These Women to Breaking Point?" *Me, Myself & I* (Nov. 16, 2017), http://www.refinery29.uk/world-news-anxiety-twitter-facebook

23. "Brief Diversions Vastly Improve Focus, Researchers Find," *Science Daily* (Feb. 8, 2011), https://www.sciencedaily.com/releases/2011/02/110208131529.htm

CHAPTER 6

1. "The 2017 State of Telecommuting in the U.S. Employee Workforce," FlexJobs (accessed December 2017), https://www.flexjobs.com/2017-State-of-Telecommuting-US/

2. Bruce Daisley, "Ease Off Those Emails and Smartphones When You're at Work, Says Twitter Boss," *The Times of London* (Sept. 29, 2017), https://www.thetimes.co.uk/article/ease-off-those-emails-and-smartphones-when-youre-at-work-says-twitter-boss-w6dg6kdxg?shareToken=77567a582775te8tb1402e1b02f6257a

3. V.C. Hahn and C. Dormann, "The Role of Partners and Children for Employees' Psychological Detachment from Work and Well-Being," *Journal of Applied Psychology*, 98(1), 26–36, APA PsycNET, http://psycnet.apa.org/record/2012-28973-001

4. *The Future of Work and Death* (2016), directed by Sean Blacknell and Wayne Walsh, http://www.imdb.com/title/tt5142784/

5. SWNS, "Half of Millennials Have a 'Side Hustle,'" *New York Post* (Nov. 14, 2017), https://nypost.com/2017/11/14/half-of-millennials-have-a-side-hustle/

6. Thomas Costello, "How to Pursue Your Passion and Launch a Side Hustle," GoDaddy (April 10, 2017), https://uk.godaddy.com/blog/pursue-passion-launch-side-hustle/

7. Mark Molloy, "CEO Praised for Wonderful Response to Employee's Mental Health Email," *The Telegraph* (July 12, 2017), http://www.telegraph.co.uk/health-fitness/mind/ceo-praised-wonderful-response-employees-mental-health-email/

8. Helen Leggatt, "Mobile Workers Sleeping with Their Smartphones," *BizReport*, (May 30, 2011), www.bizreport.com/2011/05/mobile-workers-sleeping-with-their-smartphones.html

9. "Virgin's Richard Branson Offers Staff Unlimited Holiday," BBC (Sept. 24, 2014), http://www.bbc.co.uk/news/business-29356627

10. Joe Lazauskas, "Why More Tech Companies Are Rethinking Their Perks," *Fast Company* (Oct. 16, 2015), https://www.fastcompany.com/3052329/why-more-tech-companies-are-rethinking-their-perks

11. Anne Perkins, "Richard Branson's 'Unlimited Holiday' Sounds Great—Until You Think about It," *The Guardian* (Sept. 25, 2014), https://www.theguardian.com/commentisfree/2014/sep/25/richard-branson-unlimited-holiday-job-insecurity

12. Suzanne Moore, "It's Not a Perk When Big Employers Offer Egg-Freezing—It's a Bogus Bribe," *The Guardian* (April 26, 2017), https://www.theguardian.com/society/commentisfree/2017/apr/26/its-not-a-perk-when-big-employers-offer-egg-freezing-its-a-bogus-bribe

CHAPTER 7

1. Stefan Stern, "Why Have Job Titles Become So Complicated?" *The Guardian* (Oct. 5, 2017), https://www.theguardian.com/commentisfree/2017/oct/05/job-titles-bbc-identity-architects

2. Timothy Ferriss, *Tribe of Mentors* (London: Vermilion, 2017)

3. Cathy Engelbert and John Hagel, "Radically Open: Tom Friedman on Jobs, Learning, and the Future of Work," *Deloitte Insights* (July 31, 2017), https://dupress.deloitte.com/dup-us-en/deloitte-review/issue-21/tom-friedman-interview-jobs-learning-future-of-work.html

4. Bruce Daisley, "The Way We're Working Isn't Working" [podcast], *Eat Sleep Work Repeat* (May 22, 2017), http://eatsleepworkrepeat.com/secret-creativity/

5. Madeleine Dore, "Why You Should Manage Your Energy, Not Your Time," BBC (June 13, 2017), http://www.bbc.com/capital/story/20170612-why-you-should-manage-your-energy-not-your-time

CHAPTER 8

1. David Goldman, "Facebook Claims It Created 4.5 Million Jobs," CNN Business (Jan. 20, 2015), https://money.cnn.com/2015/01/20/technology/social/facebook-jobs/

2. Lisa Miller, "The Ambition Collision," *The Cut* (Sept. 6, 2017), https://www.thecut.com/2017/09/what-happens-to-ambition-in-your-30s.html

3. Katty Kay and Claire Shipman, "The Confidence Gap," *The Atlantic* (May 2014), https://www.theatlantic.com/magazine/archive/2014/05/the-confidence-gap/359815/

4. "Young Women Facing Career Confidence Crisis, with 23% of Those Currently without a Mentor Seeking One for Advice and Skills Development," Monster (2015), http://info.monster.co.uk/young-women-facing-career-confidence-crisis/article.aspx

5. "Pregnancy and Maternity Discrimination Forces Thousands of New Mothers Out of Their Jobs," Equality and Human Rights Commsion (July 24, 2015), https://www.equalityhumanrights.com/en/our-work/news/pregnancy-and-maternity-discrimination-forces-thousands-new-mothers-out-their-jobs

6. "How Do I Ask to Change My Working Hours?" Working Families (July 30, 2014), https://www.workingfamilies.org.uk/articles/flexible-working-a-guide-for-employees/

7. Kim Parker and Wendy Wang, *Modern Parenthood*, "Chapter 1: Changing Views about Work," Pew Research Center (March 14, 2013), http://www.pewsocialtrends.org/2013/03/14/chapter-1-changing-views-about-work/

8. Christina Lemieux, "Agencies Need to Harness the Power of Part-Timers," *Campaign* (March 14, 2017), https://www.campaignlive.co.uk/article/agencies-need-harness-power-part-timers/1427177

9. Jonathan Heaf, "How to Spot: the Slashie," *GQ* (Oct. 15, 2017), http://www.gq-magazine.co.uk/article/how-to-spot-the-slashie

10. Bill Yenne, *Julius Caesar: Lessons in Leadership from the Great Conqueror*, Palgrave Macmillan, 2012

11. Steve Heighton, "Digital Distraction Is Bad for Creativity," *The Walrus* (Nov. 30, 2017), https://thewalrus.ca/digital-distraction-is-bad-for-creativity/

12. Jean M. Twenge, "Have Smartphones Destroyed a Generation?" *The Atlantic* (Aug. 3, 2017), https://www.theatlantic.com/amp/article/534198/

13. Vivek Murthy, "Work and the Loneliness Epidemic," *Harvard Business Review* (September 2017), https://hbr.org/cover-story/2017/09/work-and-the-loneliness-epidemic

CHAPTER 9

1. Caitlin Moran, "My Posthumous Advice for My Daughter," *The Times* (July 13, 2013), https://www.thetimes.co.uk/article/my-posthumous-advice-for-my-daughter-qkjgh7whg9l

2. Lee Price, "How to Be the Person People Want to Talk to at Networking Events," Monster, https://www.monster.com/career-advice/article/networking-advice-tips-0816

3. Mercedes Cardona, "The Future Is Automated for the People, According to Webby Trend Talk," Velocitize (Oct. 26, 2017), https://velocitize.com/2017/10/26/webby-awards-wpe-summit-this-automated-life/

4. Amber van Natten, "How Journalist Ann Friedman Built a Newsletter Empire," NewsCred (March 31, 2015), https://insights.newscred.com/how-journalist-ann-friedman-built-a-newsletter-empire/

CHAPTER 10

1. Dan Kadlec, "Is It Rude to Talk about Money? Millennials Don't Think So," *Money* (Jan. 21, 2016), http://time.com/money/4187855/millennials-money-manners/

2. Rachel Krantz, "How to Get a Raise No Matter What, According to Businesswoman Cindy Gallop," *Bustle* (Dec. 16, 2015), https://www.bustle.com/articles/129373-how-to-get-a-raise-no-matter-what-according-to-businesswoman-cindy-gallop

3. Manoj Arora, "7 Income Streams of Most Millionaires," LinkedIn (Nov. 1, 2015), https://www.linkedin.com/pulse/7-income-streams-most-millionaires-manoj-arora

4. James Pratley, "The Side Hustle: Kodes Accessories," Starling Bank (Oct. 4, 2017), https://www.starlingbank.com/blog/the-side-hustle-kodes-accessories/

5. Charlotte Cowles, "Will I Ever Have Enough Money?" *The Cut* (Nov. 10, 2017), https://www.thecut.com/2017/11/money-mom-will-i-ever-have-enough-money.html

6. Josephine Cumbo, "Saving for Retirement: How Much Is Enough?" *FinancialTimes* (Nov. 16, 2017), https://www.ft.com/content/8e324baa-c86f-11e7-ab18-7a9fb7d6163e

INDEX

ACKNOWLEDGMENTS

Firstly, a huge thank-you to the Andrews McMeel Publishing team. Kirsty, I will always remember fondly how and where we happened to meet! Thank you so much for your enthusiasm and support and the way you champion new ideas. Allison, thank you for being such a fantastic editor. I am so lucky to be working with someone as smart as you.

Thank you to my literary agent, Abigail Bergstrom, for making my publishing dreams come true. Massive thanks to Diving Bell, my brilliant management team. Kim Butler and Justin Girdler, it's a joy to work with you both every day.

Thank you to all the magical multi-hyphenates quoted inside the pages of this book for letting me interview you or letting me use your story as a case study. I am so grateful for your contribution and time.

Thank you to anyone who has ever listened to or been a guest on my *Ctrl Alt Delete* podcast. So many ideas and thought starters for the book were born out of those magical and unfiltered conversations with many different activists, creatives, and entrepreneurs, and I am infinitely grateful to anyone who continues to engage with the show and the subject matter. (If you're reading this and interested, check it out on iTunes or wherever you get your podcasts!)

Thank you to my dad—the first self-employed multi-hyphenate I ever observed and learned from—and mum: thank you for everything. Shout-out to my siblings and my best friends who give me the best advice (you know who you are). And last but not least: Paul, I love our exciting, freeing, creative, multi-hyphenate life together.

ABOUT THE AUTHOR

Emma Gannon is an author, award-winning podcaster, speaker, and *Sunday Times* business columnist who was named one of *Forbes*'s "30 under 30" in 2018. She is the former social-media editor of British *Glamour* and has been published everywhere from the *Guardian* to *Teen Vogue*. Her popular interview podcast, *CTRL, ALT, DELETE*, where she discusses work, culture, and careers with interesting people from all walks of life, has been nominated for a Webby Award and has been recommended by *Wired, Esquire, Elle, Red, Marie Claire,* the *Times*, and many more. This is her second book. She lives in London.

Enjoy *The Multi-Hyphen Life* as an audiobook narrated by the author, wherever audiobooks are sold.

Andrews McMeel Publishing
a division of Andrews McMeel Universal
1130 Walnut Street, Kansas City, Missouri 64106

www.andrewsmcmeel.com

Revised and updated from *The Multi-Hyphen Method*,
originally published in 2018 by Hodder & Stoughton (UK).

20 21 22 23 24 BVG 10 9 8 7 6 5 4 3 2 1

ISBN: 978-1-5248-5242-9

Library of Congress Control Number: 2019946555

Editor: Allison Adler
Art Director: Julie Barnes
Production Editor: Elizabeth A. Garcia
Production Manager: Cliff Koehler

ATTENTION: SCHOOLS AND BUSINESSES
Andrews McMeel books are available at quantity discounts with
bulk purchase for educational, business, or sales promotional use.
For information, please e-mail the Andrews McMeel Publishing
Special Sales Department: specialsales@amuniversal.com.